TRANSGRESSIONS: CULTURAL STUDIES AND EDUCATION

Cultural studies provides an analytical toolbox for both making sense of educational practice and extending the insights of educational professionals into their labors. In this context *Transgressions: Cultural Studies and Education* provides a collection of books in the domain that specify this assertion. Crafted for an audience of teachers, teacher educators, scholars and students of cultural studies and others interested in cultural studies and pedagogy, the series documents both the possibilities of and the controversies surrounding the intersection of cultural studies and education. The editors and the authors of this series do not assume that the interaction of cultural studies and education devalues other types of knowledge and analytical forms. Rather the intersection of these knowledge disciplines offers a rejuvenating, optimistic, and positive perspective on education and educational institutions. Some might describe its contribution as democratic, emancipatory, and transformative. The editors and authors maintain that cultural studies helps free educators from sterile, monolithic analyses that have for too long undermined efforts to think of educational practices by providing other words, new languages, and fresh metaphors. Operating in an interdisciplinary cosmos, Transgressions: Cultural Studies and Education is dedicated to exploring the ways cultural studies enhances the study and practice of education. With this in mind the series focuses in a non-exclusive way on popular culture as well as other dimensions of cultural studies including social theory, social justice and positionality, cultural dimensions of technological innovation, new media and media literacy, new forms of oppression emerging in an electronic hyperreality, and postcolonial global concerns. With these concerns in mind cultural studies scholars often argue that the realm of popular culture is the most powerful educational force in contemporary culture. Indeed, in the twenty-first century this pedagogical dynamic is sweeping through the entire world. Educators, they believe, must understand these emerging realities in order to gain an important voice in the pedagogical conversation.

Without an understanding of cultural pedagogy's (education that takes place outside of formal schooling) role in the shaping of individual identity--youth identity in particular--the role educators play in the lives of their students will continue to fade. Why do so many of our students feel that life is incomprehensible and devoid of meaning? What does it mean, teachers wonder, when young people are unable to describe their moods, their affective affiliation to the society around them. Meanings provided young people by mainstream institutions often do little to help them deal with their affective complexity, their difficulty negotiating the rift between meaning and affect. School knowledge and educational expectations seem as anachronistic as a ditto machine, not that learning ways of rational thought and making sense of the world are unimportant.

But school knowledge and educational expectations often have little to offer students about making sense of the way they feel, the way their affective lives are shaped. In no way do we argue that analysis of the production of youth in an electronic mediated world demands some "touchy-feely" educational superficiality. What is needed in this context is a rigorous analysis of the interrelationship between pedagogy, popular culture, meaning making, and youth subjectivity. In an era marked by youth depression, violence, and suicide such insights become extremely important, even life saving. Pessimism about the future is the common sense of many contemporary youth with its concomitant feeling that no one can make a difference.

If affective production can be shaped to reflect these perspectives, then it can be reshaped to lay the groundwork for optimism, passionate commitment, and transformative educational and political activity. In these ways cultural studies adds a dimension to the work of education unfilled by any other sub-discipline. This is what Transgressions: Cultural Studies and Education seeks to produce— literature on these issues that makes a difference. It seeks to publish studies that help those who work with young people, those individuals involved in the disciplines that study children and youth, and young people themselves improve their lives in these bizarre times.

Girls in a Goldfish Bowl

Moral Regulation, Ritual and the Use of Power amongst Inner City Girls

Rosalyn George
Goldsmiths, University of London, UK

SENSE PUBLISHERS
ROTTERDAM / TAIPEI

A C.I.P. record for this book is available from the Library of Congress.

ISBN: 978-90-8790-185-1 (paperback)
ISBN: 978-90-8790-186-8 (hardback)

Published by: Sense Publishers,
P.O. Box 21858, 3001 AW
Rotterdam, The Netherlands

Printed on acid-free paper

For Siobhan

With Love

CONTENTS

ACKNOWLEDGEMENTS

To the girls who lie at the heart of this study and gave generously of their time, sharing their emotions and reflections on friendship with me, I am tremendously grateful. I am also grateful to their schools, their teachers and their parents.

I am enormously indebted to Stephen Ball and thank him for his encouragement and support, his insights and reflections, his patience and understanding and his warmth and humour. I could not have wished for a better 'critical friend.'

In particular I wish to thank Carol Fox, Naima Browne and Jac Ashton who read through my work, helped me to clarify my thoughts and constantly encouraged me to keep going. Many thanks go to Dennis Atkinson, Clyde Chitty, Debbie Epstein, Heather Mendick, Carrie Paechter and Lez Smart, all of who read or commented on parts of my work often at critical moments or junctures. Thanks to the many colleagues and friends who on a day to day basis made life easier with words of encouragement and friendly faces: Paul Dash, Sue Dixon, Jenny Griffiths, Chris Kearney, Clare Kelly, Maggie Rogers, Anna Traianou and John Wadsworth.

Finally, love and thanks to my family, particularly Siobhan, Brian, Wendy, Eddie, Keith, Finuala and my parents, John and Christine, for their continual support and interest in my work.

Thanks to all of you.

PREFACE

In the classic cultural-sociological text edited by Stuart Hall and Tony Jefferson, *Resistance through Rituals* (1980), contributors celebrated the achievement of cultural agency (literally) as the public performances of (a predominantly) masculine and sometimes masculinist social formation. Mods and rockers alike co-represented a new academic genre of sub-cultural cool as well as providing flamboyant dramatic assemblages. These creative displays were theorised as evincing the 'magic resolutions' of marginalised young (mainly white and working class) me. These subjects were newly aware of the appeals of the consumer market, which were often in contradiction to the conformist demands of education. Preferring their status in the fashion and popular cultural public arena rather than as subordinates in the labour market, young men were seen as creating their own exciting cultural worlds.

It was, in the main, a homo-social world even if this was not commented upon as such.

Indeed it was this decisive *break* from the 'femininity' of schooling and their families that strikes readers now about this work - ideologically confirming the traditional association between the 'private and personal' as a less exciting, more directly oppressive and smaller 'female' world.

However, as many feminists/ethnographers and cultural theorists have subsequently asserted (McRobbie, 1980; Skeggs, 1992), to pose the problematic this way already skews our point of interest so that the division *between* the public/private remains under-theorised, a point Stuart Hall acknowledges in later work (Hall, 1980).

The predominantly Gramscian focus of the 'Birmingham School' thus meant that, whilst the world of paid labour was not its principal concern, it nevertheless was still preoccupied by the public realm - a move that Jane Miller (1990) argued meant retaining a male-centric model of both culture and class.

If The Centre for Contemporary Cultural Studies, Birmingham thought class was a cultural accomplishment, it was a move which to some extent anticipated the burgeoning of interest in the work of Pierre Bourdieu. Yet, as it is now widely recognised, for both strands of cultural critiques – gender and 'race' complicate class.

Understanding that class might function as a psycho-social, affective and intensely moral vector of gendered experience, has accompanied a different type of theoretical and empirical attention (Skeggs, 1997, 2004; Reay, 2005).

Thus the feminist-inspired interest in that which *Resistance Through Ritual* relegated to the 'backstage', insists that the vitality and social and cultural complexity of the personal and 'private' (for example. girls' friendships) constitute crucial cultural work about 'difference'. Whilst style may still feature, what counts more are how these practices inscribe intense feelings of desire, alienation and need.

Recently feminist ethnographies and commentaries on friendship amongst girls have gained momentum. Such literature has 'corrected' the tendency to privilege the 'performative' and visible practical productions of male identity work (Fordham, 1995; Proweller, 1998).

The newer literature on girls' friendship has also to some extent powered the move to seek out a distinct piece of parallel intellectual territory called 'Girls' Studies'. Such an epistemic claim follows the logic of academic work more generally, (Bernstein, 1996). However this burgeoning of work is by now international (for example, Aapola et al, 2005) and increasingly registers the confidence of a branch of feminist intellectual endeavour that knows these 'ordinary' relations are, in effect, anything but banal, since for their subject they carry just the same level of normative significance as other forms of more socially acknowledged relations.

Rosalyn George's monograph makes a welcome addition. She has built upon the growth of literature that draws from cultural studies, a powerful analytic language, one that is able to get into the interstices of schooling, to reveal how friendship emerges as a site of power and moral regulation. She also shows what sort of femininities get done there and amplifies a trend to make identity into a 'verb' (Kehily et al (2002) & *Discourse* Special Issue on Relationship Cultures (2002); Reay, 2001).

Using an eclectic reading of previous work, George, situates her own empirical investigation and creates a vivid account of young inner city girls' inveterate concerns with establishing a sense of belonging which centre on how they negotiate a self in the matrices of their school-based friendship networks. The girls' social relations are meticulously charted. We see their struggles as part of the fraught process of girls' transfer from their primary to a more widely dispersed selection of secondary schools. These relations are revealed as sources of pleasure, pain, loyalty and difficult to overcome antagonism and as circuits of desiring to belong, fearing and being anxious about exclusion. They are inextricably linked to 'wars' of position – to how girls strive for or achieve or are allocated 'positionality' (Alcoff, 1997) in the highly charged nexus of relations. There are leaders, close allies, followers and those on the periphery, rather than simple, self-evident divisions between 'popular' or 'unpopular' girls. Interestingly, being a 'good listener' is awarded an especially important place and status in many groups.

Yet, if these relationships are preoccupying, they are simultaneously dismissed as having nothing to do with the institutional life of primary and secondary school, mainly because teachers and other professionals (as well as mothers) conspire to deny, naturalise or dismiss them. Moreover, the public discourse of 'nice' femininity presents obstacles to the girls' own capacity to reorder and contest, what are 'private' friendship arrangements, such as the everyday dynamics of making (or breaking) social arrangements. However, being 'left out' or ignored by girls who were once one's friends is, as the author shows, a particularly devastating form of emotional manipulation.

Since dissention is seen in tension with 'nice' white middle class femininity, the excluded or 'teased' girl is not in much of a position to complain. This, rather than any natural passivity, is what tends to obscure girls' ability to publicise the emotional harassment, which circulates as part of the static of power strategies which some girl leaders can stage-manage to their own ends. Being a 'bully' is theorised not as a separate identity but one that is often deployed by the girl who has mobilised enough capital (ability, attractiveness, confidence) to claim the position of being the 'leader' of the group.

However, as I have noted, if it is obvious that the underworld of girls' schooling is a fraught business, highly social as well as highly structured with its 'rules and rituals'. The author shows these discourses and practices of friendship are (almost) completely disconnected from adult knowledge.

So whilst they evince a whole set of important consequences for the girls, their educational success, their social ease (or lack thereof), their school choices and their ability to be reflexive of their social circumstances, the 'grown-up' world consistently misrecognises and misreads them.

Patiently building a closely recorded (and well-listened to!) ethnographic picture of the girls over many years, Rosalyn George tracks her sample into and across the transition from primary school to their respective and contrasting secondary schools. She is able to build up trust and reflexivity, weaving into her portrait a sense of her own investments in the project which unites her commitment to equity and to seeing schooling and education as sites of power and contestation, not confined to issues of the curriculum or in the rhetorics and indeed the realities of teachers' own moral valuing of social diversity.

One of the most plangent aspects of the study is the extent to which attention is paid to institutional policies valuing London's much-vaunted diversity in terms of speaking of the need for equity, but there is no professional discourse or ability to engage with girls about their own inequitable struggles as they seek claims for respect and recognition in that part of their lives which founds (or confounds) their sense of social worth.

This study will remind women readers of their own girlhoods perhaps and maybe alert us to thinking of how boys 'do friendship' in similar or different modes.

We urgently need to make 'cultural studies' speak to 'educational studies' and the book shows just what can be gained in understanding once we situate the subject in the pulse of her own lived experience. There is a massive explanatory loss that occurs when we decontextualise social policy from the ethnographic and 'felt' texture of living schooling. George shows just what an absorbingly cultural, as well as achievement-oriented, activity this is for many girls and the complexities and contradictions such achievements install.

We have to ask what is it that compels many educational professionals to 'see' education (especially secondary and beyond) as devoid of the affects, concerns and rites of passage that enthral their pupils. This type of detailed work reveals what it might be that we see if we redirect our attention. Since in showing how the interpersonal world is negotiated via working with (and perhaps questioning) moral norms, Rosalyn George's monograph is a powerful response to Andrew Sayer's (2005) important argument that we need to make more sense of how people invest in and prioritise moral norms.

It seems to me that studies such as Rosalyn George's reveal the force of his argument because she demonstrates how the seemingly inconsequential aspects of friendship have a moral valence/violence that traverses the 'standards agenda', 'the respect agenda' and the 'diversity agenda'.

It might not to be too strong to claim that unless we listen more to what Rosalyn George's global city girls say about their friendship, we will have a very distanced view of them. We may well miss how central to their sense of a possible self is 'growing up' in, and as, the symbolic and moral regulation of the feminine forms of friendship.

One might even push further and question the conventional conceptualisation of the subject as the singular self, rather than what the book implies and others argue, that subjectivity is wrested more in a context of all those 'others' who we both imagine and form as an audience for putting into question the illusion of our unique authored identity.

INTRODUCTION

There is a growing body of literature exploring the nature of girls' friendship in schools (Hey, 1997; Quicke and Winter, 1991; Nilan, 1991). The majority of this literature, however, has focussed on girls in their 'teen years', i.e. those of fourteen years old and beyond. Traditionally, girls' friendship groups have been characterised by teachers, parents and educational researchers as 'malicious, bitchy, catty and resentful' (Davies, 1979, p. 65), with boys' friendships being seen as far more straightforward (Nilan, 1991). This book challenges these familiar characterisations through highlighting the cultural practices that underpin urban girls' friendship groupings and their social networks. It will explore the emotional and social dynamics of a group of inner city preadolescent girls and their friendship groups as they transfer from primary school to secondary schools. Within this transitional phase of schooling, much of the existing work on girls' friendship has focused on girls' collaborative work in groups, adult-child relationships and girls' willingness to conform to school structures and organisations. This book explores such ideas but goes further in that it exposes some of the complex processes by which urban girls' friendships are constructed and sustained.

This book presents an in depth exploration of pre-adolescent girls' friendships as they relocate from their inner city state primary school to their secondary schools. The schools are all urban[1] schools and represent the state and public sector of education. The girls in the book encompass the diversity of ethnicities found in large urban communities and how the girls manage and negotiate their friendships across ethnic divisions is central to the book.

Critical moments in the girls' schooling are analysed to explore how cultural shifts impact upon existing power relations. Through discussion, interviews and journal entries of the girls and their teachers in one primary school and six secondary schools, the book provides an insight into the organisation of friendship groups, the rules which govern group membership, and the role groups play in defining the quality and nature of the girls' relationships and their social networks at school. By focusing on the constitution of the groups, questions of 'leadership' and 'popularity', 'race' and ethnicity and 'bullying' are interrogated and their resonance for the 'exclusionary' and 'inclusionary' practices which characterise the friendship groups, are considered. The disparity between the priorities of the girls at the point of transfer and the priorities of the school as a learning institution is also documented. The book highlights the emotional investment girls make in their friendships, and makes more visible this aspect of their lives in their day to day interactions in the classroom and in schools.

The rationale for this book came from a realisation that patterns of inclusion and exclusion were a regular feature of young girls lives and that this widespread social experience was on the whole socially invisible and that where it was observed its importance was denied or diminished. Furthermore this book highlights what might be called the bleak side of young girls' social relationships, and attention to this has provoked some unease amongst readers of my work. Some of the responses I have met when talking about this work have been: 'not all girls are mean', 'girls are wonderful'. One mother I spoke to was distressed at the prospect of her child either being a 'horrible, nasty leader' or 'a victim' who will be 'bullied' and 'miserable'. It has been suggested that I should provide a more nuanced portrayal and that it is unfair to only highlight this negative aspect of girls' lives. Such comments have caused me some anxiety for it would be a grave mistake for any reader of this book to interpret my study as a condemnation of girls and women. On the contrary, I wish to make it clear that my deep affection for girls has been the driving force behind this project. Western culture has long affirmed the niceness of girls and therefore this study, which provides another perspective and a different lens through which to make sense of girls' lives, can possibly be unsettling. However, I would wish that the insights this study brings will have some impact upon those adults working with young girls, be they school teachers, youth workers or adults from others agencies, in raising awareness of the emotional investment girls make in their friendships, and to make more visible this aspect of their lives in their day to day interactions in, for example, the classroom, the school or the youth club.

Throughout this book, the names of the girls, their mothers and the schools they attended have been changed to maintain their anonymity.

ORGANISATION OF THE BOOK

The book is divided into two parts. The first part is concerned with the theoretical underpinning of the empirical work and the methodology and methods used to generate the data. For those readers who may like to read the data first, I suggest they go straight to Chapter 4 before returning to the theoretical and methodological chapters at a later stage. I outline the chapters in more detail below.

Part A

Chapter 1   Understanding Friendships: A Critical Review.

This Chapter serves to set the context for the rest of the book. It will provide a rationale for the book through a critical examination of how friendship has been constructed in various historical, social psychological, sociological and cultural accounts of friendship. Further, through exploring the literature on friendships, the book highlights how the majority of studies of friendship have been extrapolated from empirical work done on boys at school. The book reveals the lack of attention within social research that has been paid to issues of pre-adolescent girls leading to a view that friendships where they are viewed as a homogeneous. Misconceptions about 'friendship' are explored. This chapter will also document how both 'race' and ethnicity have been absent from much of the literature on friendship.

Chapter 2   Themes and Issues

This Chapter outlines the conceptual framework adopted in the study. It traces my journey as a feminist researcher and illustrates how it has informed my thinking about equity issues and feminism in particular. For this book, I have combined elements of feminist post-structuralism and 'relational psychology' as these approaches offer ways for discovering how the girls in the study develop accounts of themselves as friends and their relationships to each other. These approaches also assist in developing an understanding of how the regulatory practices of the girls' teachers and their schools have an impact on the operation of the girls' friendship groups. The Chapter discusses the degree to which girls' behaviour in contemporary society is socially ordered and controlled within the friendship groups and how far this is framed by expectations, rules and rituals of femininity. The Chapter will also show how the girls are positioned between two conflicting discourses; one where they are publicly affirmed and rewarded for displaying feminine qualities of sensitivity and care, and secondly where they have to respond to the demands to succeed in school and beyond, by putting their own desires for autonomy first. The work of the relational psychologist alongside a post-structural interpretation has been useful for mapping changes in the girls' subjectivities at the time of transition from primary school to secondary school. I also draw attention to the tensions and contradictions as well as the possibilities and limitations that arise from working with these two approaches.

Chapter 3   Researching into Girls' Friendships

The Chapter details the methods employed in the field and the methodological and ethical issues that surfaced in researching young girls' friendships. Throughout the Chapter, I pay attention to issues of power and control, which I show are neither easy nor clear. I emphasise that working with pre-adolescent girls makes it even more important to continually exercise reflexivity in terms of power relations and ethics. In this Chapter will I describe the locations and schools where the research was carried out and introduce the girls who are the focus of this study and their mothers to the reader. The process of data collection and the process of data analysis will also be discussed.

Part B

Chapter 4   Inner City Girls Talking About Friendship

Through foregrounding the girls' voices, this Chapter illustrates the dilemmas that the girls face in trying to understand and respond to constructions of friendship idealized by the culture of the school and wider society. This Chapter also explores the ways in which characteristics of friendship are played out and experienced within the context of the school. In discussions of the girls' accounts, I analyse the extent to which understandings and patterns of friendship change between their primary years and their early years of secondary school, alongside a consideration of how ethnicity may be involved in these changes. A reflection on the 'negative' side of friendship forms part of this Chapter, through examining the conflation in some of the girls' narratives and the paradox that a friend can also be a bully.

Chapter 5   The Internal Dynamics of Girls' Friendship Groups

In this Chapter the girls' express powerfully their thoughts, perceptions and views on what is happening within their friendship groups in relation to issues of stratification, status and power. By focusing on the constitution and nature of the friendship groups, its structure is explored. Questions of leadership are also considered through an analysis of common understandings of popularity amongst the girls. The Chapter also discusses the complex relational work that the girls who form the inner circle of the friendship group have to engage in, in order to secure their position within the group hierarchy alongside a consideration of those girls located on the periphery of the friendship group. The Chapter will examine how the girls' teachers, both wittingly and unwittingly, contribute to the maintenance of group hierarchies within the friendship groups and sustain the leadership within them.

Chapter 6   Transferring Schools Transferring Friends

This chapter explores the issues and concerns that impact upon urban girls' friendship groups as they transfer from primary to secondary school. Through an examination of the literature on transition, the book will demonstrate how the majority of studies have focused on the structural and organisational aspects of transfer, with very few acknowledging the importance of friendship within the process. The huge diversity of provision of secondary schools found within an urban setting and the implications this has for choice at 11+ and the girls' subsequent friendships are explored. The Chapter will show how friendship is a central concern for the girls at this point in their schooling. It will document the extent to which urban girls' existing social relationships are disrupted as they adapt to and engage with a new school setting.

Chapter 7

In this Chapter I focus on school choice and the impact this has on the girls' friendships. In particular I focus on the experiences of Shumi and Leila and their mothers. Both girls are from minority ethnic backgrounds and both have invested in school success. Through discussion, interviews with the two girls, the girls' mothers and their teachers, plus journal entries made by the girls, critical moments in the girls' schooling are analysed to explore how cultural shifts impact upon existing power relations amongst the girls, their teachers and their friends. The girls' choice of school and their mother's interventions in the choice process are explored alongside the way the girls' approach new friendships. Issues around 'truth telling', 'racelessness' and complicity are examined.

Chapter 8   Conclusion: Bringing it all together

This Chapter will summarise the book's main findings by highlighting key themes for the girls and their friendship networks; leadership, popularity, bullying and 'race'. It will highlight how issues of 'race' are managed by the girls and how they work against homogenisation of school processes which would be found in both suburban and rural settings.   The Chapter shows how the girls are positioned between two conflicting discourses; one where they are publicly affirmed and rewarded for displaying feminine qualities of sensitivity and care, and secondly where they have to respond to the demands to succeed in school and beyond by putting their own desires for autonomy first. The Chapter will critically evaluate the implications of these findings for a reassessment of how girls' friendships within an inner city context are seen and understood by teachers and schools and the wider society in general. The Chapter will highlight some broader research questions that remain to be addressed in future work.

NOTES

[1] The use of the term urban in the context of this book relates to the multi-ethnic, multi-cultural, inner city London schools the girls attended and the impact that the diversity of provision that accompanies inner city schooling had on the girls friendship.

PART A

PART 2

UNDERSTANDING THE CULTURE OF GIRLS' FRIENDSHIP GROUPS

A CRITICAL REVIEW

Grace is waiting there and Carol, and especially Cordelia. Once I am outside the house there is no getting away from them. They are on the school bus, where Cordelia stands close beside me and whispers into my ear: "Stand up straight! People are looking!" Carol is in my classroom, and it is her job to report to Cordelia what I do and say all day. They're there at recess and at lunchtime. They comment on the kind of lunch I have, how I hold my sandwich, how I chew. On the way home from school I have to walk in front of them, or behind. In front is worse because they talk about how I'm walking, how I looked from behind. 'Don't hunch over' says Cordelia. 'Don't move your arms like that.' They don't say any of the things they say to me in front of others, even other children, whatever is going on is going on in secret, among the four of us only. Secrecy is important, I know that; to violate it will be the greatest, the irreparable sin, if I tell and will be cast out forever. But Cordelia doesn't do these things to have power over me because she's my enemy. Far from it, I know about enemies. Cordelia is my friend. She likes me, she wants to help me, they all do. They are my friends, my girlfriends, my best friends. I never have had any before and I'm terrified of losing them.
(Atwood, Cats Eye, 1988, p. 119-20)

The evoking of a past through an interaction with the present provides the rationale and context for this book. Memories of a subordinated girlhood in the pursuance of 'friendship' which, painted out by a brighter and wiser adulthood, has been reawakened by observing the painful investments made by daughters and their 'young friends' in attempting to belong and be accepted by others. My memory is of course fractured by time and shaped by the present, but that such a painful and emotional investment in friendship continues to preoccupy not only adolescent girls but also those of a very young age, decade upon decade, is troubling. The kind of concern revealed by Margaret Atwood's quotation (above) is pivotal to this book, and illustrates the importance of relationships and connection in girls' lives, along with the fear of solitude, which lead many to hold onto destructive relationships, even at the expense of their emotional safety. In Atwood's novel, Emily, who is bullied by Cordelia, the 'popular' girl, knows that by staying friends with her she will be cared for at times and under circumstances beyond her control. Emily's fear of losing her friends leads to her silent acceptance of what appears to be unacceptable behaviour. Such silence is woven into the fabric of the female

3

experience and in the hidden culture of girl's friendship groups, the façade of intimacy often hides the anguish and psychological pain that friends may and often do inflict upon each other. The complex interactions that characterise the friendship groups of many girls highlight some of the key themes for this book.

Girls' troubled friendships in their primary schools have warranted little serious attention from their teachers or other adults who perceive the 'breaking' and 'making' of friendship as an inevitable and almost a 'natural' and routine part of their daily classroom experiences and, furthermore, over so quickly that intervention is unnecessary. In the view of this 'naturalism', girls' friendship groups have traditionally been characterised by teachers, parents and educational researchers as 'malicious, bitchy, catty and resentful' (Davies, 1979, p. 65), with boys' friendships seen as far more straightforward (Nilan, 1991). In the secondary phase of schooling, much of the current work on girls' friendships challenges such stereotypes and is concerned with exploring the complex processes through which friendships are constructed and sustained. Researchers (Hey, 1997; Nilan, 1991) have dismissed the simplistic characterisations and instead highlighted the deft and sophisticated cultural practices, which underpin friendship groupings and their social networks. In contrast, existing work on primary-aged children has focused on collaborative working groups, adult child relationships and girls' willingness to conform to school structures and organisations. I shall challenge the assumptions upon which the latter are based.

This book is about the friendships and the friendship groups of pre-adolescent girls. It is about how such girls understand and negotiate friendship within the context of their primary and the early years of their secondary school. I shall explore the meanings that the girls attach to the intimate behaviour and social experiences that are important in their lives. Such meanings are created within the culture of their own friendship groups and whilst these groups revolve around the culture of adults, that is parents and teachers, they primarily exist for themselves.

Within the context of urban multi-ethnic and inner city primary and secondary schools, I will analyse the factors that affect the development and structure of girls' friendship groups and the effects the girls' position in their friendship group has on their developing sense of identity. I will highlight the tensions and contradictions within the girls' relationships and the power and opportunity they reproduce. The book is an attempt to portray the intimate social world of pre-adolescent girls from their point of view. The girls in this study represent the ethnic and cultural diversity found in large urban communities.

In searching for understandings to make sense of the young girls' experience of friendship there is a developing literature on girls and their friendships; however there remains a paucity of material on primary aged girls. One of the problems therefore in theorising issues related to the experiences of these younger girls' friendships has been finding conceptual frameworks that acknowledge their complexities, for girls at this young age do construct distinctive friendship cultures. The majority of texts on girls' friendships (Hey, 1997; McRobbie, 1991; Gilligan et al., 1990; Lees, 1986), although invaluable contributions to the sociology of friendship, all, with the exception of Gilligan's work, deal exclusively with adolescent secondary school girls. It is this neglect of work on girls' friendships in their primary school and early years of secondary school that this book will address.

STUDYING FRIENDSHIPS

Traditionally, the way educationalists and indeed psychologists have framed issues relating to children's friendships has allowed essentialist notions of masculinity and femininity to predominate. Girls are positioned as conforming, compliant and responsive to an imposed moral and indeed ethical order. As Adler and Adler observe:

> *In contrast to the boys' defiance, girls become absorbed into the culture of compliance and conformity. They occupy themselves with games and social interactions where they practice and perfect established social roles, rules and relationships. Not only do they follow explicitly stated rules, but they extrapolate upon these, enforcing them onto others as well.*
> (Adler and Adler, 2001, p. 209)

Within these studies there has been a tendency to oversimplify how young children construct their friendships. Adult views and understandings are transposed onto children's' voices and psychologists then attempt to construct universal paradigms and precise and unambiguous definitions of complex and often contradictory phenomena. Furthermore, a real sense or acknowledgement of social change is absent from their approach. Friendship is taken to be an ahistorical social phenomenon unaffected by social context or cultural shifts.

It is only recently that research into friendships in school has been explored through the lens of sociological analysis. Sociological work, mainly a male preserve until the late 70's (Haralambos, 1995, p. 581), had meant that women's issues of any category were rarely studied until the 70's. Thus, many of the earlier sociological studies of friendship focused exclusively on boys, e.g. Willis, 1977; Corrigan, 1979; Fine, 1981.

In this Chapter, I will trace various perspectives that have been employed in the attempt at understanding girls' friendships. These approaches are not chronological, nor sequential, nor are they mutually exclusive. The different perspectives can be organised into the following broad headings:

- Social psychological constructions of friendship.
- Philosophical accounts of feminine friendship.

- Sociological and cultural studies approaches.

SOCIAL PSYCHOLOGICAL CONSTRUCTIONS OF FRIENDSHIP

Social psychologists tend to take an approach to human social behaviour which emphasises factors within a person, and also the social environment, as well as the interaction between an individual and the environment. Their goal is almost always to arrive at empirical 'findings'. The vast bulk of the literature on friendships emanates from the field of social psychology. On the whole, this literature points to the importance that children place on socialising with each other, with arguably unsurprising findings, that children with friends are seemingly more socially competent and less troubled than children without friends (Hartup, 1983). Indeed Corsaro (1985) specifically points to the peer group as the most significant public realm for children, with friendship seen as a valued and normative state. However, not all friendship is the same; gender segregation is identified as a factor in friendship groupings, with girls and boys demonstrating distinct cultures strongly tied to the experiences that they share with their friends (Kutnick and Kington, 2005).

With developmental psychology, until recent times, as the dominant model in the search for understanding children's progress and maturity, much of this work suggests that friendship develops through a series of stages, from common interests to mutual recognition and liking (Bigelow and La Gapia, 1980; Rubin, 1985; Steinberg, 1986). Hartup's (1996) work presents friendship as providing an important source of cognitive and social frameworks. Frones (1995), notes that most theories of social development regard childhood as a psychological process out of which the adult personality is formed. Further, the stages assume that childhood, whilst progressing through phases of social development and influenced by social and cultural factors, is nevertheless dependent on innate cognitive and biological foundations. Piaget is often a key resource in these psychological conceptions of the child and their social relations. Piaget, a major proponent of stage development theory in his "genetic epistemology" (Piaget, 1965), links the biological facts of immaturity to the social aspects of childhood. He advances four stages of cognitive development during which children's thinking undergoes patterned changes as they mature biologically and gain social experience. However, he fails to acknowledge the impact of the social upon a child's development; the child is universal, an undifferentiated psychological being, outside society and outside history. Furthermore, developmental models have been unable to take account of differences in 'race'[1] class or gender and the possibility that children develop through these stages in different ways and at different rates. They also work with a conception of childhood that is simply a phase on the road to the adult world, rather than childhood as a social and cultural construct in its own right.

However, one of the most recently forged social psychological frameworks is social constructivism. Social constructivism is part of the social interactionist perspective. The foundation of this theory is the belief that children are active agents in their socialisation and that socialisation is a collective process involving parents, the market and state, leading to childhood being a socially constructed category. Nonetheless, Thorne (1993) points out that this still 'defines children primarily as learners, as those who are socialized, who are acted upon more than acting. Beneath this view lies a double standard; social scientists grant adults the status of full social actors, but they define children as incomplete, adults-in-the-making'. Thorne continues to emphasise that 'socialization' and 'developmental' models assume that outcomes of social practices are known and that children will develop into conventional adults with appropriate masculine and feminine traits unless the process 'slips'. She maintains that such approaches: 'distort the vitality of children's present lives to continually refer them to a presumed distant future' (Thorne, 1993, p. 3).

In contrast, Denzin (1977) argues that socialisation is not a: 'structurally determined process whereby the values and goals of social systems are instilled in the child's behaviour repertoires' (Denzin, 1977, p. 2-3), but rather, he emphasises the tension between structure and agency[2]. However, in his attempt to employ a social interactionist perspective to explore the secret world of the child, he, like the developmental psychological accounts that preceded his work, concluded that the child became social by becoming adult. In all of this the child is a not- quite social being, not- quite socially competent, and thus transparent to researchers and adults generally. For as adults, it could be argued, we know all we need to know about children, having been there ourselves.

As noted already, most of the findings from work done by developmentalists have been generalised to all children with little distinction made between class or 'race' or gender. However, where gender has been acknowledged as a variable in understanding friendships, gender differences are explained through essentialist notions of masculinity and femininity. A clear example of this is provided by Kolhberg's (1978) study into the ethical thinking of young people. His research, which was carried out over a period of twenty years, studied only boys between the ages of four and sixteen. Kohlberg used his findings to construct a six-stage development process and, although he did not include women in his research, he claimed that this staged development was universal to all. Women, he maintained, were only able to attain level three stage because the higher levels of understanding of morality were contingent upon greater participation in the public sphere of life, a forum which, on one hand, excludes women whilst, on the other, denigrates and penalises the private sphere they occupy. In failing to take account of the women's experience, Kohlberg declares the male as the norm and up to point three in this staged model, what is true for men is also true for women (Paechter, 1998). Kolberg's assumption that women were incapable of moving beyond this stage has to remain unsubstantiated since they were absent from his research. This absence resonates with Walkerdine's critique of Darwin's rationale for men's superior intellectual powers over women's [3].

... of course it is not a new trick to subtract the feminine to render it worthless and in so doing to count girls out. Charles Darwin demonstrates for us how easily the slippage is achieved from the idea of men's superior attainment to their greater mental capacities.
(Walkerdine, 1988, p. 10)

PHILOSOPHICAL ACCOUNTS – MORAL DEVELOPMENT

The work of Carol Gilligan (1982) and her colleagues has challenged the male orientated theories of moral development. In arguing against gendered accounts like Kohlberg's, she suggests: 'that "the justice voice" of moral theory and male-based moral development is not the only way in which people conceptualise moral problems' (Paechter, 1998, p. 73). Gilligan proposes that if one 'begins with women's lives and develops constructs from their experience, moral problems arise from conflicting responsibilities rather than rights; this requires a different mode of thinking, one that is contextual and narrative rather than formal and abstract' (Gilligan, 1982, p. 19). She differentiates between a 'self' that is defined through separation and a 'self' delineated through connection. The theoretical basis of her work lies in a belief that women's relationships are born out of a desire for attachment to, and connectedness with, each other. She argues that women, in being 'othered' by male theories of moral development, have instead found alternative moral voices. Gilligan's psychoanalytical work places women at the centre of the research process and, by listening to women's voices, she builds theory and moves away from the traditional psychological approaches, which promote an individualistic view of development, towards a socio-cultural analysis.

Gilligan and her colleagues are 'in essence reframing psychology as a practice of relationship, by voicing the relationships that are at the heart of the psychological inquiry' (Brown and Gilligan, 1992, p. 22). For me, the importance of Gilligan's work is its articulation with the continuous conflict that girls face over being good to themselves, whilst at the same time being good to others, and this possibly offers another way of thinking about the relationship of connectedness to individualism.

Adolescence poses problems of connection for girls coming of age in Western culture, and girls are tempted or encouraged to solve these problems by excluding themselves or excluding others, that is, by being a good woman or by being selfish... for girls to remain responsible to themselves they must resist the conventions of feminine goodness; to remain responsible to others, they must resist the values placed on self-sufficiency and independence in North American culture.
(Gilligan et al., 1990, p. 9-10)

The central themes that Gilligan, Lyons and Hamner (1990) identify in the stories told by the women and girls in their study, reflect truth, goodness and survival. These are also the reoccurring concerns expressed by the girls in my study. However, where this work diverges from that of Gilligan's is in relation to her conception of young primary aged girls as confident and self-assured. For the primary girls here, such confidence was context specific, e.g. Taheera only becomes confident when Anisha, the group leader, is not at school, suggesting that although assurance and confidence are social achievements, they are not always socially possible, and not available to all girls in the same way and to the same degree. Carol Gilligan's work has been criticised by many feminists for its focus on the experiences of middle class white girls. Chapter 2 discusses these critiques in detail.

Gilligan's study, nevertheless, provides an insightful and refreshing basis for a consideration of other studies concerned with examining the moral ordering amongst girls and their friends. Here Nilan's (1991) work has a particular resonance with the young girls in this book. Although her research focused on adolescent girls in Australia, their acknowledgement that their friendships were contingent on the development and sharing of a mutually recognised moral order was the view reflected by the girls in my study, who also understood that adherence to a certain moral code was a necessary part of successful friendships. However, my research also brings into question the policing within groups of this moral code. It would seem that the code was not always democratically constructed on the basis of mutual trust, but through the domination of the leader. How the leader positions herself as 'powerful' within the group remains a vexing question and leads to a consideration of sociological accounts of children's friendships and peer relations.

SOCIOLOGICAL ACCOUNTS OF FRIENDSHIP

Sociological critiques of developmentalist perspectives, for their adherence to individualism and their abstract conception of friendship, are fairly recent. Troyna and Hatcher (1992), whilst arguing that staged theories like that offered by Piaget need to be rendered more social, do see these earlier theories as useful and a valuable source for researching children's lives.

Sociologists, however, have until recently tended to marginalize the subject of childhood. The reason for this lack of interest could be, as Ambert (1986) suggests, the interest that the founding fathers of sociology had in macro issues that were framed through male experience, thereby relegating women and, by extension, children to the margins of sociological research.

Sociological studies of friendship have, however, emphasised that gender is the most significant of social factors in shaping friendship patterns. Despite this, female friendship has received such little attention that some question whether it exists at all or whether women have the capacity for it, suggesting that women lack the bonding instinct that binds men together in groups (Tiger, 1969). The cultural assumption that men and women do friendship differently has been sustained by an adherence to the view that men are thought of as having a great propensity for friendship. Men are seen to be more active in work and leisure and thereby able to generate a larger network of friends for example, at the pub, the golf club or on the football terraces. Women's friendships on the other hand are seen as being far more tenuous and characterised by petty squabbles and jealousies. Their friendships are supposedly less stable and there is a strong imagery about women being 'bitchy' to one another, gossiping and betraying confidences (Allan, 1989). There are numerous examples of this portrayal of women to be found in literature ranging from Jane Austen to Jackie Collins, on television, especially in Soap Opera, and in 'Girls' own stories, for example the 'My Best Fiend' series. Angela McRobbie's (1991) analysis of the girls' weekly journal Jackie depicted girls as never being able to trust another woman unless she was old and 'hideous', in which case she wouldn't appear in the stories. Sue Lees (1986), however, observes that there is a gradual change in the representation of female friendship in literature and suggests that one of the many positive advantages of black women's fiction is the placing of women's friendships centre stage and the positive depiction of female friendship. Lees provides the example of Toni Morrison's novel Sula, where friendship between two women is portrayed as special and different, and argues that friendship has never before been depicted as the major focus of a novel. Publishers are also now catering for a whole range of books where heroines are depicted as more independent and capable of friendship with both boys and girls, examples of this can be found in the stories of Gene Kemp (1977) and Jacqueline Wilson (2000). Men and boys, however, rarely read such books and thus entrenched gendered views of friendship remain unchallenged.

Many sociologists (Henry, 1963) have appropriated commonsense understandings of friendship and have transposed these views and understandings onto their constructions of boys' and girls' friendships. They suggest that boys, like men, have larger networks of friends than girls, who are typically portrayed as having dyadic or triadic relationships. Within this sociological perspective, boys enjoy sharing activities and doing things together, whereas girls' friendships are emotionally closer, more expressive, equal and fair with a focus on the relationship itself. Henry maintains that:

> *As they grow towards adolescence, girls do not need groups; as a matter of fact, for many things they do, more than two is an obstacle. Boys flock, girls seldom get together in groups of four, whereas for boys a group of four is almost useless. Boys are dependent on masculine solidarity within a relatively large group. In boys' groups, the emphasis is on masculine unity; in girls cliques the purpose is to shut out other girls.*
> (Henry, 1963, cited in Lees, 1986).

The data arising from this study challenges Henry's assumption that girls have no need for groups. The data, whilst supporting conceptions of closeness and care, also found girls operating within large networks of friendships. Indeed, the hierarchy within the girl's friendship networks, rather than consistently providing support, did also marginalize and at times exclude girls. In addition, the unquestioned decision making by Isobel, Carol, Anisha and Melody, the powerful leaders, certainly challenges assumptions that girls' friendships are equal and democratic.

As discussed earlier, on the whole, girls' same-sex relationships have been overlooked in sociological studies of peer relations. Like the psychological accounts referred to earlier, early ethnographic studies of youth culture which focused on boys have attempted to construct theorisations, but have failed to acknowledge that these studies provide highly gendered accounts. Many accounts of girls and schooling have been extrapolated from empirical work done on boys at school, with gender being absent from such analysis. Or, as in Paul Willis's (1977) highly celebrated account of young men negotiating school and the work place, girls are seen through the eyes of 'the lads' as objects to be possessed. As Arnot (2002) observes, Willis's 'lads' by celebrating their masculinity and sexuality through an anti-school culture, and by positioning the hard working boys as 'effeminate' or 'cissies', inverts 'the hierarchical distinction between mental over manual labour by transposing it to the hierarchy of male and female' (Arnot, 2002, p. 51). These accounts unreflexively take on the male's eye view of the social world and social relations. Girls are objectified and either ignored or mystified. By attempting to insert girls into these sociological and cultural accounts, the gendered nature of such work remains unproblematic and masculinist constructions of youth culture remain dominant (Hey, 1997).

Even so, some feminist critiques of the state and schooling have allowed for a focus on girls and their experience of schooling. These critiques have granted girls a space to be heard and recognition of agency. Many of the studies, however, focus on adolescent girls. Llewellyn's (1980) study showed how girls are influenced by stereotypical images of sexuality, which regulates how girls should look and behave, whilst Leonard's (1980) research exposed the shifting pattern within girls' friendships once boyfriends were introduced.

From the early 1970's to the present, McRobbie has been one of the major protagonists in researching girls. Her work highlights the pressure exerted on girls 'to achieve idealised expectations of femininity', a theme that is very visible within the data here. McRobbie's research has been concerned with exploring the influence of popular culture on girls' behaviour at school and within their friendship group or subculture. Her studies were prompted by the lack of attention paid to gender by male sociologists, leading to an overestimation of the conformity of girls to the norms and values of the school and the wider society. McRobbie's work illustrates how girls, and working class girls in particular, have always been involved in resistance to these expectations, but their concerns have been eclipsed by the work done on boys. In her study of the 'Mill Lane Girls', McRobbie (1978) points out how the working class girls formed a distinctive sub- culture, which distanced them from the middle class girls who they called 'swots'. They were also critical of their dress sense and their taste in boys. McRobbie found a major schism in her work, for the girls in her study, whilst focusing heavily on the acquisition of getting a 'fella', did at the same time want to resist the inevitability of marriage, children and home by subverting the dominant notions of femininity as mediated by the school, which were about being academically successful, bourgeois and nice. Within these studies of girls, their difference is explored and sometimes celebrated in terms of femininity. Femininity has a dual function in feminist theorising as a condensate of oppressions and as a site of resistance.

Other aspects of femininity have been explored by Walkerdine (1990), who suggests that girls, by engaging in popular culture, internalise conceptions of what it is to be feminine. Such a construction plays out a message telling girls they have to be 'good' and 'selfless' and resonates with Gilligan's work which demonstrated that a girl's desire for emotional connection is a key signifier of femininity and source of support. Both Walkerdine and Gilligan's work illustrated that the practice of femininity through friendship comes at a social cost. Being good and selfless is an impossible ideal which, as Walkerdine observes, can be resolved by projecting badness from the self onto others (Walkerdine, 1990).

It is Valerie Hey's (1997) groundbreaking study which most thoroughly critiques and problematises the simplistic sociological and psychological accounts of girls' friendships, and that resonates most closely with my own work. In her study, Hey demonstrates how complex, contradictory and fragmented girls' relationships with each other are, and how at best friendship can be a contradictory process, where girls learn that 'accommodation, survival and resistance' can take place to the social pressures and discourses of femininity that surround them (Oliker, 1989, p. 170). Hey focuses on the patterns of power within these relationships and how these patterns of power operate within the girls' social networks. These patterns of power are a major interest in my work. Hey's study points to the enormous amount of emotional energy that girls invest in their friendships and the pain and anguish experienced by the girls when things go wrong. The inclusionary and exclusionary dynamics of the friendship groups are closely explored resulting in an 'under the skin account' of friendships which are characterised by secrecy, intimacy and individual girls' struggles to 'fit in'. Hey's study demonstrates how negotiating friendship is hard emotional labour, complex and intense and that the significance of girls' friendships demands further analysis.

All the above studies, undertaken by feminist scholars, focus exclusively on adolescent girls and, as indicated earlier, there have been very few studies of same-sex friendship amongst younger girls. Of those available, there is a clear reflection of the work of Gilligan. Although Gilligan's work has been much contested the recognition that connection and caring are key markers of femininity, and therefore carry systems of meaning, allows for girls' friendships to be studied in the context of a particular sort of social action. Meyenn's (1980) study of schoolgirl peer groups found the peer group to be the dominant organising principle in the social life of the 12/13-year-old middle school girls. Meyenn saw friendship as a central and visible part of the girls' school lives, but argued that there was fluidity within the peer groups in the sense that there was no clear leader or role of leader in evidence. Meyenn suggested that equality is a defining characteristic of girls' peer groups and that this was related to the: caring and supportive role of women in our society, i.e. the girls' peer group may act as a particular kind of socialising agency within capitalist societies that produces women who prefer not to compete with men (Meyenn, 1980, p. 141). My work challenges Meyenn's, for in the friendship groups studied there was a clear leader alongside different roles taken on by other members of the group. A recent and fascinating paper by Kehily et al (2002) explores the private world of pre-adolescent girls aged 9 -10 and their investments in friendship and femininity. The paper suggests that the group of girls engage in the process of producing themselves as 'girls' and as 'friends' through the medium of talk. However although the paper demonstrates how girls are discursively situated within the broader context of the school, it fails to acknowledge the power relations that operate within the particular group of girls and how such power may shape and mould understandings of friendship and femininity. Without such an analysis of power, Kehily uncritically assumes that the production of friendship through talk, takes place within a democratic and egalitarian forum. It fails to acknowledge how words can be used as weapons which wound, resulting in girls retreating into silence rather than risking the potential pain of being excluded either, physically or emotionally (Brown and Gilligan, 1992). Thorne (1993) cites the work of Hughes (1988) whose research into girls playing 'four square' found that the girls competed in a co-operative mode and used the language of 'being friends' and 'being nice' while aggressively getting others out so that their friends could enter the game. Hughes maintains that the girls did not experience 'nice' and 'mean' as sharply dichotomous, but simply manoeuvred their rhetoric and expressed nuances through mixed phrases, like 'nice mean' and 'not really mean'. Hughes' study, whilst acknowledging the quiet aggression of the girls, fails to give adequate attention to how girls experience 'nice' and 'mean', and therefore I would argue can only give limited meaning to understanding how they experienced their friendship. This study suggests that the powerful members of the group will invest as much energy into appearing 'nice' both to adults and in front of adults as they will spend damaging an individual's self esteem, retreating beneath a surface of sweetness to hurt the less powerful girls in secret.

'RACE'

The assumed universality of friendship, lacking differentiation and context, has resulted in very few studies of either African-Caribbean or Asian girls' friendships. Indeed: 'Generalizations about 'girls culture' come primarily from research done with girls who are class–privileged and white: the experiences of girls of other class, 'race' and ethnic backgrounds tend to be marginalized' (Thorne, 1993, p. 102). Studies of African-Caribbean girls, however, do suggest that girls can find ways of achieving academic success without conforming to many of the goals and values of the school, and through avoiding serious conflict with authorities by well-measured deviance (Fuller, 1980; Mac an Ghaill, 1988; Gillborn, 1990; Mirza, 1992). Drawing on Anyon's (1983) concept of 'resistance within accommodation', Mac an Ghaill (1988) explores the strategies adopted by a group of young black women friends, to deal with their experiences in a sixth form college. These 'Black Sisters', as he called them, adopted a highly instrumental approach to their schooling, which was anti school but pro – education:

The Black Sisters in responding to their schooling in terms of a strategy of resistance within accommodation provide evidence in the British context to support Anyon's insightful suggestion. On one hand, they reject the racist curriculum; on the other, they value highly the acquisition of academic qualification. Theirs is a strategy that is both anti-school but pro education. (Mac an Ghaill, 1988, p. 11).

Mary Fuller also focused on the experiences of a small number of black girls, arguing that they formed a recognisable subculture within the school. Fuller argued that this subculture was based on their experience of being black and female and that, whilst these girls gave the outward appearance of being disaffected with school, interviews with Fuller suggested that they had a positive image of their own ability and pursued academic qualifications as a public statement of their capabilities.

A further study by Farzana Shain (2003) on the schooling and identity of Asian girls shares a degree of correspondence with the findings from this study. One of the groups of girls in Shain's research formed an all–Asian friendship group to avoid attacks and abuse at school, but this group also became involved in activities which ran counter to the dominant values and culture of the school. Another group in her study prioritised educational advancement and sought to avoid trouble at all costs (Shain, 2003, p. 81). Shain's work has some resonance with the way African-Caribbean and African girls discussed in Chapter 7 of this book responded to school.

For the African-Caribbean girls in this study, their friendships which had crossed both class and 'race' boundaries whilst at primary school became exclusively 'black' after transferring to secondary school. For these girls, identity politics often took precedence over friendship, with their friendship group, like Mac an Ghaill's 'Black Sisters and Mary Fuller's girls, functioning to support each other in achieving academic success within an environment they perceived as hostile. The girl's valued assertiveness and direct conflict, and this resistance to conventional understandings of femininity, like Mc Robbie's Mill Street Gang, was misunderstood and misrepresented as an anti-school orientation by both the girls' classmates and their teachers. However, like the girls in Carla O'Connor's (1997) study of African American High School students, this group of girls expressed a high degree of racial consciousness and their friendship operated through a 'collective', affirming for each other their affiliation to their African-Caribbean community and also a commitment to academic success.

Their knowledge of struggle did not curtail their academic success but may have facilitated their sense of human agency and facilitated their academic motivation (O'Connor, 1997, p. 593).

It is interesting that these accounts of African-Caribbean girls' friendships parallel those of the 'lads' in their outward focus, pointing out the different labour market opportunities in Britain for girls (and boys) from minority backgrounds and their subsequent effect on aspirations and orientation to schooling.

Other girls in my study, those of African origin, rather than being confrontational in their relationships to teachers and school, evolved a more complex response, which involved keeping a low profile, subscribing to the values of the school and being detached from their resistant peers. Signithia Fordham's research (1988) into the conflict that high achieving 'black students' experience between 'making it' in school and identification with black culture resonates with this group of girls. Fordham's study found that the characteristics required for success within the school system contradicted those of solidarity with black culture, resulting in the girls developing a strategy of 'racelessness'. This 'racelessness' is evident in the girls' commitment to the 'values and norms' condoned in the school context, as well as their rejection of the features of the black community which run contrary to the values of the school, for example speaking non-standard English, commitment to group advancement rather than individualism. Thus the individualism necessary for achievement in school resulted in the girls putting a distance between themselves and their black peers and entering into friendships, which would maximise their social and academic mobility. Fordham suggests that for these girls: 'They do not believe - nor does their experience support - the idea that they can be truly bi-cultural...Instead their experiences both in and out of school, support the value of appearing raceless to their teachers (and friends) and other adults in the school context' (Fordham, 1988, p. 83). However, for Leila, the African girl in this study, whilst her commitment to the 'values' and 'norms' of the school led her to adopt the 'racelessness', which Fordham describes, this 'racelessness' was only evident in school and amongst her school friends. Within her own black community, Leila and her family were actively involved. The experiences of the African-Caribbean girls and those of Leila underlines the importance, not only of comparing the differences between ethnically diverse groups, but exploring difference within them as well.

CLASS

There has been little work undertaken which has examined the links between girls friendships and social structures. Valerie Hey's (1997) work illustrates how girls' school friendships were 'coded and were entangled within the densities and intensities of social division' (Hey, 1997, p. 125). Studies of popularity, as distinct from friendship, amongst adolescent girls have found that the socio economic status of the girls' family background is highly influential (Thompson, 2002; Hey, 1997; Eder and Sandford, 1986). In this study, class features primarily in the diverse make up of the core group of girls, which includes both middle class and working class girls, For this group, at the primary school level, there tended to be a general flattening out of class differences and there was a relative invisibility of class distinctions, which resulted in the girls from less affluent backgrounds being integrated into the peer group. Social class in this study did not determine the girls' friendship group; they were a high achieving group of girls who were supported by both their teachers and their mothers, mothers who, irrespective of their social and economic background, were aspirational regarding their daughter's academic success.

CONCLUSION

This Chapter demonstates the lack of attention within social research to the issue of pre-adolescent girls' friendships. An examination of the literature on friendships has demonstrated how the majority of studies on peer relationships and friendships have focused on boys with many accounts of girls extrapolated from this empirical work and with gender being absent from such analysis. These accounts have unreflexively taken on the male's eye view of the social world and social relations, with girls being objectified or ignored or mystified.

There have however been some accounts of adolescent girls and their social relationship, for example, Hey (1997) and McRobbie (1978), nevertheless until recently there have been very few studies of same-sex friendship amongst younger girls and, in contrast with those of the older girls, many of these studies have focused on collaborative working groups and girls' willingness to conform to school structures and organisations, with little account taken of the complexities of these younger girls' friendship patterns.

Throughout this Chapter, I have referred to particular writers, for example, Gilligan, Walkerdine, Davies and Hey, whose work and theorisations I will draw upon throughout this book, as their work has particular significance for the findings arising from this study. These findings will show that the ways in which children are positioned or choose to position themselves within their friendship groups are informed by dominant discourses of femininity and their daily social interactions.

NOTES

[1] ' Race' is put into inverted commas to emphasize that 'race' is a socially constructed term.

[2] Structure/agency theory is a now recognised as a branch of social theory that reconciles the debate between whether social structure or social agency should be given theoretical primacy - by refusing to grant theoretical primacy to either. Structure/agency theorists suggest that social agents are inherently socialised and that the actions of agents are informed by and shaped by social structure such as norms and institutions prevalent in the society they are socialised into. On the other hand, the actions of actors may, individually or collectively, alter and shape social structure such as norms and institutions.

[3] The chief distinction in the intellectual powers of the two sexes is shewn by man's attaining to higher eminence, in what ever he takes up, than can woman....if men are capable of a decided pre-eminence over women in many subjects, the average mental power in man must be above that of a woman (Darwin, Charles, 1896, p564)

CHAPTER 2

GIRLS, POWER AND DISCOURSE

Empirically this study is located within sociological research on friendship. As described in Chapter 1, this research is about how pre-adolescent girls negotiate their friendships and how they position themselves or are positioned by the discursive practices they engage in. Conceptually I have drawn on two bodies of work to develop my theoretical framework, feminist post-structuralism[1] and the relational psychologists' work, as the most useful in exploring and interpreting the data. To some extent however this Chapter is a retrospective account, for whilst my own autobiography has led me to favour a feminist post-structuralist[1] position for understanding how the girls' negotiated their friendships, the way I have also come to know girls' friendships and how they function in groups has arisen out of the data itself. Glaser and Strauss's (1967) concept of grounded theory suggests that theory should develop out of social research and that it should be generated from the data that are collected. They are critical of theory that is superimposed upon data and reject conclusions arrived at from an a priori assumption.

In this Chapter, I explore both the theoretical positions I have outlined above and draw attention to the tensions and contradictions that arise from working with these two approaches. I start with some autobiographical excerpts, and illustrate how they have informed my thinking about equity issues and feminism in particular. These excerpts describe how I have been influenced by feminist post-structuralism as a theoretical resource which I have found useful in explaining how the girls in his study take up their positions in relationship to one and other. This first section of this chapter concentrates on these concepts as abstract notions as they have evolved theoretically. I then turn to consider the body of literature, which has engaged with how girls and boys come to know themselves as feminine and masculine, drawing on the relational psychologists' work of Carol Gilligan and the Harvard school. Appropriating from post-structuralism, I will then explore discourse and power as explanatory tools and discuss the importance of Foucault's work as interpreted and employed by feminist post-structuralists for this study.

AUTOBIOGRAPHICAL EXCERPTS: PERSONAL STATEMENT

There are many contexts for conducting research and one of those is the personal / political narratives and discursive positioning of the writer. Jane Miller (1995) describes the importance of starting research from the 'autobiography of the question'. I have, in Chapter 1, already alluded to how my own painful experience of primary school provided me with a passionate drive to research the area of pre-adolescent girls' friendships. In this section, I want to look at how my schooling and entry into higher education have produced my own investments in narratives of equity, and the position from which I understand the processes of fairness and empowerment in relation to class, gender and 'race'.

Throughout my professional life, an agenda, which places the promotion of social justice at its core, has provided the *raison d'être* for my work. My experiences of a girl being raised in a working-class Irish Catholic family, where responsibilities and roles were ascribed to members of the household on the basis of their gender, was my initiation into an understanding of how patriarchy operated as the dominant ideology in society and the organising principle by which all were supposed to live their lives. My primary school years served to sharpen my understandings, where it seemed that boys, purely through 'birth right', had access to resources both material and human which most of the girls were denied. It was also at primary school that I learnt about racism. Teachers' anger and hatred was not only directed at the 'coloured' children in the school, although they were few and far between, but also at the children of Irish labourers. Both my brother and I were beaten by teachers; my first experience of corporal punishment and public humiliation was at the hands of Miss Johns, I was five years old at the time. My brother may have deserved his beatings, but I certainly didn't. I was heavily investing in producing myself as 'a good girl' (Walkerdine, 1990) trying to be industrious and unassuming. I was good at reading, writing and arithmetic and as I moved through the school as a fairly high achieving girl, I felt able to attach myself to the 'good girls group'. This came at a price, for, like the girls in this study, I and some others were often excluded from their ranks.

A move to an academically orientated all girls secondary school, which was facilitated by my passing of the 11+ examination, focused my attention on issues of class, where favour and privilege was meted out to those who 'fitted the bill'. Coming from a working class background I very quickly learnt my place amongst peers and friends whose class location and access to wealth was something that I could barely imagine. Many of my friends came from 'professional 'families where going to university was an unquestionable part of their lives. Within a year I had moved from being a high achiever at primary school to a low achiever in this highly academic and middle class environment. Much of the work of the early sociologists of education for example Basil Bernstein, Michael Young, Nell Keddie, resonates profoundly for me regarding aspects of access to knowledge, as mediated through the cultural and value systems of the school.

A degree in sociology provided a framework for trying to make sense of these macro and micro inequalities which characterised societies. In terms of gender, at the micro political level my attention was drawn to Kate Millet's (1970) argument that the personal is political, where women's groups reconstructed male-defined political action by organising on an anti-elitist and collective basis, with a commitment both to the importance of personal experience and to direct political action. As a sociologist my reading of the debate as documented by Ann Oakley (1972), with its emphasis on the distinction between the biological sex of the female and male compared with the socially constructed gender of feminine and masculine, assisted in the structuring of my thoughts and responses. Indeed the theories proffered by the socio-biologists, where the female should take on the primary role of child care since they were the ones that gave birth, had a powerful effect on my feminism. Such a position seemed to me to be imbued with a patriarchal ideology in its most basic form by arguing that one's biological sex determines one's social and cultural characteristics and roles.

Juliet Mitchell's (1971) work was particularly influential at this time and focused my attention on the composite nature of feminism and its varying strands, e.g. Marxist feminism, socialist feminism and radical feminism. Mitchell's work attempted to highlight how different feminists identify different causes of women's inequality and hence different ameliorative strategies. She argued that women, in addition to challenging biological oppression, needed to identify and analyse three other structures; women's role in economic production, sexuality and its regulation and control, and the socialisation of children. What Mitchell highlighted was that the perpetuation of male power over women was and is a complex phenomenon.

My interest in gender politics was consolidated during my MA in Sociology, a time of debate regarding the theoretical and political agendas of many feminists. I attempted to grapple with the pulls and struggles of this debate where the old meta-narratives, such as Marxist feminism and radical feminism, gave way to an emerging discourse of deconstruction, expounded by writers such as Stanley and Wise (1993). Deconstructivist commentators fragmented macro-analytical concepts, for example gender, 'race' and class. In relation to gender they questioned the validity of grand narratives and encouraged a suspension of belief in universal truths. They argued against the essentialism that defines the dichotomous categories of men and women, boys and girls, instead maintaining that there are various overlapping discourses of femininities and masculinities that vary over time and across cultures. Walby summarises post-structuralist contentions as 'The notion of 'women' and 'men' is dissolved into shifting, variable social constructs which lack coherence and stability over time' (Walby, 1992, p. 34). However, post-structuralist theorists have been criticised for their over concentration on the concepts of 'woman' and 'man'. According to many post-structuralists, the signifiers 'woman' and 'man' do not equate with actual women and men (Walkerdine, 1990, p. 62). Much of the work of post-structuralists problematises the relationship between actual women and 'woman' and men with 'man'. Indeed, Cowie (1978) suggests that the signifier 'woman' is not coterminous with women. In addition, post-structuralists theorists have been criticised for exaggerating the variability of the terms 'woman' and 'man'. Obviously 'woman' and 'man' (that is to say 'women' and 'men') find form in many discourses, but I do acknowledge

Walby's contention that there remain discernible shared experiences based on gender. Walby argues that; 'The signifiers of 'woman' and 'man' have sufficient historical and cross-cultural continuity, despite some variation, to warrant using such terms'.
(Walby, 1992, p. 36).

The concept of patriarchy, which originally was understood as 'rule by the father' or 'paternal right' and has been used by feminists to describe the historical dominance of men over women, has also been criticised by some post-structuralist thinkers (Pringle and Watson, 1992; Stanley and Wise, 1993) for its essentialist connotations. They maintain that it is an essentialist concept, for it unifies women's oppression in relation to men and fails to account for the differences between women based on 'race', class and sexuality. Yet many feminists would suggest that it is erroneous to abandon the concept of patriarchy in the face of women's widespread experience of male domination. There is indeed some opposition to post-structuralist pronouncements. Walby, for example, maintains that there are 'sufficient common features and sufficient routinized interconnections for it to make sense to talk of patriarchy' (Walby, 1992, p. 36).

White middle-class women have been rightly criticised for portraying their subjective experience as normative for all women. However, some feminists, including myself, continue to believe in certain commonalities among women, although not authoritative or total, that cut across racial and class boundaries. Stanley and Wise note that '...at this point in time in Western culture, women do share certain kinds of socially constructed attributes and are subjected to and by men...' [original emphasis] (Stanley and Wise, 1993, p. 211). Similarly, although Pringle and Watson do not believe in a unifying identity among women, they acknowledge some shared experiences among them:

> *While we reject such notions of 'identity', we do believe that, along with continuing inequalities at every level, women have in common a discursive marginality. 'Woman' is only knowable in so far as she is similar to, different from or complementary to 'man'* (Pringle and Watson, 1992, p. 68).

My concern, along with many feminist theorists, was that if there is an acceptance that there is no unit category of woman or girl, then how are we to analyse gender relations in society? Maggie Maclure (2003) observes how many researchers, who are persuaded by post-structuralism, argue that:

> *Founding categories – woman, race, class – are saturated with effects of power and prejudice, and that productive social change will not take place if these terms are kept beyond question.* (Maclure, 2003, p. 181).

In her highly influential book Gender Trouble (1990), Judith Butler asks:

Can we refer to a 'given sex' or a 'given gender' without first enquiring into how sex and gender is given, through what it means? And what is 'sex' anyway? Is it natural, anatomical, chromosomal, or hormonal, and how is a feminist critic to assess the scientific discourses which purport to establish such facts for us? (Butler, 1990, p. 215).

Thus, do women need to be conceptualised in some other forms? That grand narratives, such as those relating to the dichotomous categories of women and men, boys and girls, have been rendered questionable is good in one sense in recognising the diverse nature of gender identities; in another it is destabilising, since post-modern and post-structuralist feminist alternatives seem equally unstable (Acker, 1994, p. 57). Francis argues that the post-structuralist's focus on 'deconstruction rather than construction can result in political nihilism and fatalism' (Francis, 1998, p. 12). It could be argued, however, that the dismantling of the category 'women' does not mean dismantling it in the sense that it does not exist, rather, on the contrary, it means dismantling the category in the sense that we know what it consists of. Thus it is the category 'not women' that we are dismantling. Deconstructing the unitary and universal category 'women' effectively means the opposite, namely the category 'woman' needs to be constantly reconstructed with rigour in order that we know precisely to whom we are referring when we use the term 'women'. How we refer to women as a category is important.

Judith Evans (1995, p. 11) also highlights the problems associated with using the term 'women'. In her writing she endeavours to distinguish between different groups of women; white, middle class, heterosexual women, such as herself, she refers to as 'we' or 'us'; black, working class and lesbian women are denoted as 'they'. Though not explicitly post-structuralist, Evans highlights the subsuming consequences of the term 'women'. Social commentators need to be circumspect in the way individuals and groups are constituted and labelled. My argument is that post-structuralist feminism can offer a more rigorous way of conceptualising the specificities and simultaneous commonalities between and among women. Stanley and Wise appear to encapsulate this concomitant sentiment when they state that

'...the category women needs deconstructing in order to focus on ontological separations as well as similarities' (Stanley and Wise, 1990, p. 33-34).

Just because there are many different types of women, it does not follow that we cannot talk about 'women'. Just as there are many feminisms, it does not mean that we can no longer talk about feminism. The category 'women' necessitates a new reading in the same way as plurality necessitates rigour. Plurality does not mean nihilism. For many, the rejection of post-structural theories comes about because post-structuralism itself seems to reject tangible categories and offer nothing in their place. It would seem that the advancement of post-structuralist theory rests upon a need to move from a deconstructivist analysis of the constitution of women towards a reconstitutive narrative. Before I go on to consider the feminist theories

23

that emerge as the most apposite to this study, I shall briefly survey and critique sociological/constructivist theories of gender.

DOING GENDER: BECOMING TO KNOW ONESELF AS FEMININE AND A GIRL

Sociology has had a long history of accounting for and describing gender differences by studying in detail the actions and practices of everyday life. Goffman (1976) describes gender displays that are highly ritualised and expressed as masculine or feminine, for example, the way a male or female walks, the way of sitting on a chair, the way the head is held or tilted. He argues that these gender displays are socially scripted dramatisations of the particular culture's idealised form of what it is to be masculine or feminine. The work of West and Zimmerman (1987) suggests that 'doing gender' is undertaken by men and women whose competence at producing themselves as culturally correct versions of masculinity and femininity is affirmed. They argue that every member of society is required to portray their gender in everyday activity, in the clothes they wear and how they talk and express themselves. So powerful is this need to conform to these cultural expectations that in western cultures, men and women, boys and girls are derided or socially excluded if they practice gender inappropriate behaviour.

From their earliest years children have been shown to hold strong views about their gender positioning (Davies, 1990; Thorne, 1993) and that their gender identities are actively constructed throughout schooling. Weedon (1987) identifies three main strands of thought which seeks to explain gender differences: scientific, psycho social and historical. This study sees gender as 'constructed' in a culture where a collection of symbols are invested with meanings that define what it is to be male and female (Ortner and Whitehead, 1981). Gender is not something people 'are' but something people 'do'.

People 'do' gender in different ways in different cultures. They are taught to learn from birth to behave in gender appropriate ways in all activities and practices of their daily lives. Indeed, they learn gender so well that they can 'do' it without even thinking consciously about doing it (Cherland, 1994, p. 11).

Cherland (1994) cites Mehan and Woods (1975, p. 143), who suggest that gender is a reflexive activity and they provide an example from the work of Garfinkel (1967), who describes the experiences of a 19 year old male who chose to dress and live and pass as a female. The person called Agnes found that being a woman and being accepted as a woman required ceaseless social performance. Agnes found that she was constantly involved in socially structuring situations in which she could engage in the practices of being female, for after living as a male for 19 years, she had to learn the routine practices her women friends had unconsciously engaged in for many years. Although Agnes remained anatomically male she lived in the world and was accepted as a woman. What her life suggests is that one is made a man or a woman within the social order by virtue of the practices one employs.

The concept of socialisation, however, has been roundly criticised for failing to take account of social change. It presumes that there is an established set of relationships which shape and mould children into being either a boy or a girl and that the relationships are fixed and unchanging. The assumption is that we develop and form an unchanging sense of self through a socialisation process, which enables us to undertake our appropriate roles in society. Clearly such an argument in contemporary society is neither appropriate nor convincing, for example, the loss of the manufacturing base, a traditional site where physical strength was a pre-requisite for employment, alongside the entry of women into the workforce in increasing numbers facilitated by new technologies, has disrupted generally understood definitions of masculinity and blurred the polarities in traditional working patterns between men and women.

Britzman (1993), along with many feminist scholars, (Davies, 1989; hooks, 1990; Biklen and Polard, 1993)) describe gender as the social construction of sex: 'what we have come to identify as belonging to men or women's behaviours, attitude, presentation of self, and so on is produced by social relationships and continually negotiated and maintained within cultures' (Britzman, 1993, p. 2). Britzman explains: 'social constructivists argue against the view that identities are stable, natural, or unique. Individuals, they argue, are not the sole authors of themselves, but rather are authored in language and by social practice' (Britzman, 1993, p. 32). Davies (1989) further argues that socialisation theories render the child without agency and a passive receiver of socialisation with a fixed identity. In this study the changing and shifting identity of the girls and their friendship groups was a result of a process of continuing negotiation with each other and also with the dominant values of the school system as mediated through their teachers.

GIRLS AND AUTONOMY

The work of Carol Gilligan (1990) and her colleagues confronts the issue of gender roles and argues that male gender identity is threatened by intimacy, while female gender identity is threatened by separation. They account for these gender differences in terms of the early relationship between mother and child. Gilligan's work reflects Nancy Chodorow's (1978) highly influential study on mothering. Chodorow's study reported that girls and boys develop different 'relational' capacities and senses of self as a result of growing up in a family in which women 'mother' (Chodorow, 1978, p. 173). She argues that all children identify first with their mother and that for girls, through the development of a personal identification with their mother, a gradual learning of feminine gender takes place, whilst boys, on the other hand, have to develop a masculine gender identification in the absence of a continuous personal relationship with their father. Thus boys, in this context, develop a 'sense of what it is to be masculine through an identification with cultural images of masculinity and men chosen as masculine models' (Chodorow, 1978, p. 176). The significance of this is that boys' identification processes are less likely to be embedded in affective relations. 'Feminine identification processes are relational, whereas masculine identification processes tend to deny relationship' (Chodorow, 1978, p. 176). Furthermore, boys are expected to separate from their mothers at a young age, thus promoting an inclination towards autonomy, detachment and objectivity. Girls on the other hand remain identified with their mother, a relationship which is predisposed towards emotional interdependence manifested and characterised by caring and compassion for others (Gilligan, 1982).

Gilligan (1995) argues that as girls grow up they experience a conflict between desires for autonomy and desires for connection and that the hierarchical structure of school works against girls who are more inclined to use language to connect than to compete. Gilligan describes how 'girl after girl in her study described the paradoxical situation: that in order to make and maintain relationships, it was necessary to keep large parts of herself out of relationships. By staying out of relationships, girls also protected vulnerable parts of themselves from attack and denigration' (Gilligan, 1995, p. 201). It is important to note that Gilligan's work is based on self-reports that provide important insights into how girls perceive their roles and relationships. Gilligan's methodology, while documenting sets of beliefs, does not examine how girls might actually negotiate such sets of beliefs. This study addresses how, within the girls' friendship groups, the girls' behaviour was socially ordered and controlled; it further investigates how negotiations amongst the groups were framed by the expectations, rules and rituals of femininity. Within the group, the available roles for girls were functional to the stability and coherence of the group. The girls were faced with the dilemma of being good and selfless, taking responsibility for others' welfare and being sensitive to their needs, or being positioned as bad and selfish where they put their own desires for autonomy first.

Adolescence poses problems of connection for girls coming of age in Western culture, and girls are tempted or encouraged to solve these problems by excluding themselves or excluding others – that is, by being a good woman or by being selfish .... for girls to remain responsible to themselves, they must resist the conventions of feminist goodness; to remain responsible to others, they must resist the values placed on self-sufficiency and independence in North American culture (Gilligan et al., 1990, p. 9-10).

These tensions, as highlighted in Chapter 1 and explored in great detail in both Chapter 4 and Chapter 5 were very pronounced amongst the girls in this study. They were in constant negotiation between responsibility for others and sensitivity to their needs, with the autonomous independent action and attention to their own needs and desires.

This study discusses the emotional complexities of the girls' friendship patterns, and shows that the emotional investment the girls make in their friendships as of greater importance than the values of the autonomous learner promoted by the school (Chapter 6 discusses this tension in detail). Nevertheless, the girls were all high achieving and success, as defined by the institution of the school, was important to them. This could suggest that the girls were in constant negotiation between the desire for personal autonomy and a sense of duty and responsibility to others within their group of friends. What the work of Gilligan highlights are the problems that girls face in how to gain some freedom in a society where caring and dependence are seen as attributes of femininity and that girls who behave in competitive and selfish ways are infringing the dictates of femininity.

McLeod (2002) observes how Gilligan's work has been roundly criticised by several feminist scholars for its universalising and essentialising tendencies (Davies, 1994; Hey, 1997). She reminds us of the dilemma facing feminists in repudiating Gillligan's work on theoretical grounds, for such dismissal does not account for why her work has such popular appeal and such purchase among so many women.

Whilst it can be argued that a Western culture of individualism may exacerbate the dilemma for women and girls of being selfless and being selfish, McLeod suggests that gender reform programmes in Western countries have opened up possibilities for personal success and public achievement and thus had an important impact on the desires and aspirations of young girls.

The emotional connectiveness and the value that girls and women place on friendship have been publicly celebrated, and virtues of care and empathy are seen as indisputable. This study suggests that the desire for intimacy amongst pre-adolescent girls engulfs them and determines their experience of schooling. The girls in this study were positioned within two conflicting discourses; one, where they are being publicly affirmed and rewarded for displaying the feminine qualities of sensitivity and care, and secondly where they have to respond to the demands to succeed in school and beyond. These two conflicting discourses place the girls in an impossible position.

McLeod argues that:

> *These twin imperatives thus exacerbate and produce new dimensions to, rather than obviate the autonomy/ connection conflict for girls. In one sense femininity is being detraditionalised through the opening up of a wider range of possibilities for girls. In another sense, femininity is being rearticulated as ideally integrating and embodying both conventionally feminine and masculine aspirations. The ideal person embraces both emotional openness and ambitions for autonomy: girls can do and be anything.*
> (McLeod, 2002, p. 11)

I would argue that McLeod here is articulating a Foucauldian clash of discourses.

POST- STRUCTURALISM, POWER AND DISCOURSE

I now turn to Foucauldian theory to extend the post-structuralist theory (discussed earlier in this Chapter) to include notions of power and discourse. Foucault adopts a wide definition of discourse, which takes into account texts, speech, architectural layout, rules and practices. Discourse refers to a system of statements, which are organised in terms of coherent rules and conventions. Power is not held so much as used in interactions and discourse, and can be productive as well as limiting. For Foucault, both knowledge and truth are produced through the vehicle of 'discourse'. In addition, Foucault argues that all identities are 'constructs' produced by socio- historic influences. In this study, the girls' narratives of friendships were central in constituting their 'reality'. As noted above, the Foucauldian concept of discourse does take into account practice, from the perspective of this study language or talk is important, in that subjectivity is primarily experienced and constructed through 'talk'. Mauthner (2002) draws our attention to the work of Hollway (1984) and Miller (1990). Mauthner describes Hollway's definition of discourse in which she links it to agency and emotions. She outlines four competing discourses for understanding heterosexuality – a male sexual drive discourse, a have/hold Christian discourse, a permissive discourse and a feminist discourse. She writes of the investment that men and women have in certain positions rather than others. Jane Miller's (1990) work on 'Seductions', in which she explores how we yield to our desires yet feel hesitant about doing so, reflects Hollway's notion of investment . Miller suggests that:

> *In trying to do justice to the complexities of women's seductions into ways of life, behaviour, beliefs and traditions which have the potential to undermine them, I have wanted to portray seduction as both multifaceted and diverse* (Miller, 1990, p. 23).

Hollway and Miller's conceptualisations are both useful for shedding light on why the girls in this research positioned themselves, or let themselves be positioned, in discourses that were damaging to them.

Appropriating from Foucault, Frazer (1988) derives her use of the term 'discourse' to incorporate language, talk and speech. She uses it in her work on schoolgirls' understanding of femininity. Frazer finds the term 'discourse' useful for understanding the variety of positions available to teenage girls or to the extent to which resistance to certain ideas is possible. Her data reflects the experience and constraints of girlhood, and how they struggle to make meaning of their class, 'race' and gendered positions. She explores the way the girls attempt to resist 'dominant meanings' or contested ideas and how they negotiate their way through different practices and accounts of their lives.

Frazer's interest in the use of 'talk' and the role it plays in constructing experience is relevant to this study for understanding the way the girls experience their relationships and position each other in contradictory ways. The girls in Frazer's study struggle over dominant meanings that exist at the level of discourse, but also in terms of their classed position. As discussed earlier in the Chapter, Francis (1996) criticises discourse analysis for its lack of attention paid to material power, however, within Davies's (1989) post-structural account of pre-school children and Hey's (1997) ethnographic study of girls friendship, power relations of class and gender are fully explored. In this book, issues of 'race' become visible through the dynamics of power operating within the friendship groups.

Christine Skelton (2001) argues that there is little agreement about what power is, or how it is constituted and, indeed, some writers (Lukes, 1986; Deem, 1994) suggest that we should give up any attempts to search for a unifying definition. I would argue, however, that the location, sources and use of power are conceptual focal points in post-structuralist theorisations. My understanding of power is influenced by the work of Foucault who suggests that power is not a possession but rather something that is passed through and mediated by persons and structures at all levels in society. He sees power as constituted through multiple and constantly shifting discourses, thus there is no truly existing duality between those with power and those without. Francis (1998) citing Jones (1997) takes issue with the position that people can actively choose to position themselves powerfully by drawing on certain discourses. My data, from the girl's interactions with each other and their teachers, would suggest that this does happen both consciously and sub-consciously. Power within this study has been shown to be present both in the relationships between the girls as explored in Chapters 4 and 5, and also between the teachers and the girls in Chapter 4. The school as an institution is explored as a powerful regulator of pedagogic practices and as discussed in Chapters 4 and 6 a site for resistance to dominant discourses of acceptable femininity, particularly as experienced by the African-Caribbean girls in the study. The African-Caribbean girls in this research, like those in Alison Jones' (1993) study of Maori girls, were at times positioned, or positioned themselves, in opposition to the prevailing discourses of femininity by being 'assertive' and 'strong' and as explored in Chapter 7 their expression of power was through 'truth telling'. This rendered them at times powerful amongst their friends and teachers, but also powerless, for by resisting the values of the school, which subscribed to dominant discourses of femininity, these girls, were positioned as difficult with behavioural problems. Following Foucault, Epstein (1993) in her book, 'Changing Classroom Cultures', situates the individual not just within discourse, but also in relation to the material realities of social construction. She argues that power hierarchies exist and, therefore, it is more difficult for some people to occupy powerful positions than others. Furthermore Epstein argues that although power is not necessarily exerted through force, but through discursive practices (in which individuals either consent or resist), she also points out that individuals may occupy positions within different and contradictory discourses. She comments:

It is, however, not always clear what constitutes consent or resistance. For example, academic success on the part of young black women in schools may

appear to be consistent with discourses of school, but can also be conceived of as resistance to discourses which places black students as 'underachievers'
(Epstein, 1993, p. 13).

Jones (1993) echoes Epstein's observation in suggesting that some positions may not be available to all girls. She describes the different sets of positions that are, or maybe, available to working class and middle class girls due to their differing material and discursive conditions. Jones (1993) cites Angela McRobbie's (1978) research on working class adolescent girls (as referred to in Chapter 1). She describes how the working class girls in her study position themselves in a discourse of femininity, which constructs successful girls as those who are attractive to men. They therefore resist the feminine subject position of the passive asexual schoolgirl and celebrate the sexualised feminine position which may secure a better future rather than chasing credentials they are unlikely to get.

Chapters 4 and 7 discusses how, for some of the girls in this study, their resistance to and accommodation of the dominant values of the school in terms of expectations of femininity reflects very clearly Epstein's observation. A more detailed discussion of the girls' resistance to the school's regulatory function is undertaken in Chapter 7.

Within the institution of the school, the teacher represents the most overt expression of power and this power is invested in her/him through the official school organisation. However, some of the teachers in this study, it could be argued, found themselves unknowingly in subordinate positions to individual girls in the friendship groups, or in opposition to the collective group in the class. Chapters 5 and 6 explore how the teachers positioned themselves or were positioned, not only by the girls in the study, but also by dominant discourses of what counts as a successful teacher.

In his work 'The Subject and Power' (1982), Foucault compares the structures of disciplinary mechanisms with institutions such as prisons, hospitals and education practices. Foucault argues that the effects of the mechanism of power are to construct individuals as subjects in two senses. First, as subject to someone else, through control and restraint, and second, as subjects tied to their own identity by their conscience and self knowledge. In this study, the operation of the friendship groups constructs the individual girls as self regulating members of the group with specific functions critical to its maintenance (this is further developed in Chapter 4). However, understandings of the friendship groups of pre-adolescent girls are complex as the power relationships between the individual girls, which are in constant negotiation within the friendship group but invisible to the outsider, cloud the issues and shape the way the friendship of pre-adolescent girls is made knowable to teachers and other adults. Foucault (1991) links power with knowledge, and argues that an individual's identity is produced through a positioning in discourses and hence through power relations. In this way, power does not exist outside of human relationships, but rather is constructed within them. Several post-structuralists have explored the construction of feminine subjectivity through discourses of domination and power in the realms of schooling. Lees (1986) study of adolescent girls illustrated the ways that teenage girls 'police' each other through language. Hey's (1997) ethnography of girls' friendship found that girls' best friendship can be both positive and negative encompassing both the nurturing aspects and 'bitchiness', especially girls' surveillance and controlling each other. The relevance and resonance of these studies for my research lies in their analysis of the parallel processes that take place where the girls in their studies both accept and resist dominant discourses of femininity.

This study, by drawing on the work of Bronwyn Davies and Valerie Walkerdine, both feminist post-structuralists working within a Foucauldian theoretical context, interrogates the identities and experiences of a group of pre-adolescent girls in primary and secondary school and to explore the practices in which their friendship groups are understood. Both Walkerdine and Davies understand post-structuralism as a positive lens through which to view the complexity and diversity of thinking about gender. They are concerned with subjectivity, which I understand as:

> *... the ways in which a person gives meaning to themselves, others and the world [...]. It is characterised by tensions and instability because it is constituted through discourses which are often in contradiction to one another.* (Banks and Davies, 1992, p. 2)

and in particular, 'the ways 'children' are 'made subject' by / within the social order and how they are agents /subjects within /against it' (Jones, 1993, p. 158).

EXAMPLES OF FEMINIST RESEARCH USING A POST STRUCTURAL APPROACH

Many feminist researchers have usefully exploited post-structuralism. Valerie Walkerdine (1981), for example, showed, in her work on power and gender in the nursery school, how boys as young as four, by making use of sexist, violent and oppressive language, can discursively position themselves as powerful over their female teacher, who becomes powerless through being rendered an object of sexist discourse. Walkerdine argues that, although the teacher has institutional power through being the boy's teacher, she is not exclusively a teacher, nor are the boys simply little boys. The boys can physically take the position of men through language and in doing so gain power. Indeed, Walkerdine's work highlights how the discourse of the school can be subverted by the boys' use of a wider discourse operating outside of the school.

Bronwyn Davies, in her account of the lives on pre-school and primary school children also adopts a post-structuralist approach. In her work she explores the processes whereby children come to know themselves as boys or girls. She argues that, children learn to take up their maleness or femaleness as if it were: 'an incorrigible element of their personal and social selves, and that they do so through learning the discursive practices in which all people are positioned as either male or female' (Davies, 1989, p. x). She argues that the presentation of 'correct' gender identity is publicly celebrated and a child who steps outside these 'norms' may be marginalized, for by challenging these 'norms' the child disrupts the gender identities of the other children in the class by 'throwing the gender dichotomy into doubt' (Francis, 1998, p. 10). In her study, Davies found that the way children negotiated gender was complex and often contradictory. She argues that children take up gender positions through the dominant discursive practices that position us as male or female. The process of discursive production happens differently for different people. The way in which individuals read and use different discourses is influenced by the degree of power they wield. Walkerdine explains how females can be affected by discourses:

> ....girls and women do not take up any position in any discourse. Their signification as girls and women matters. It means that the positions available to them exist only within certain limits. These limits are material – not in the sense that they are directly caused by the materiality of the female body, but certainly by the limits within which the body can signify in current discursive practices [original emphasis]
> (Walkerdine, 1990, p. 5).

For the girls in this book, I would suggest that some of the competing and contradictory discourses which impinged and played a role in their subject positioning were discourses of 'race', discourses of schooling and competitiveness, discourses of autonomy and individualism, discourses of collaboration and selflessness.

In her research on sister relationships, Melanie Mauthner formulates four discourses, two of which are useful for this Chapter; discourses of talk and the shifting positions discourse. She describes these as 'analytic tools for conceptualising power relations and changing subjectivity' (Mauthner, 1998, p. 79). I find these analytical tools useful for thinking about how the girls in this study occupy a range of subject positions

DISCOURSES OF TALK

Mauthner's formulation of discourses of 'talk' has relevance for this book because, within this study, it is through talk, as well as through silence and also listening, that the girls subjectivities within their friendship group are constructed and experienced. Research on gendered talk and female friendship highlight collaboration and intimate confiding as two features of girls' and women's talk.

Girls' friendships based on talk lead to specific conversational styles where they learn to create and maintain relationships of closeness and equality, criticise others in acceptable ways and interpret accurately the speech of other girls ((Maltz and Borker, 1982)). Their collaborative orientated talk, unlike boys' competitive orientated talk, maintains distinct male and female styles of interaction which continue among adults (Coates, 1993; Tannen, 1991). Interestingly, Deborah Tannen's (1991) analysis of men's and women's conversations reveals how men and women use language in different ways, women primarily to make connections and reinforce intimacy, men to preserve their independence and negotiate status. Mauthner (2002) draws attention to how the accomplishment of gender through talk, by participating in day to day social practices and interactions, becomes visible through our speech acts. Women discuss certain topics for longer than men do, share information, self disclose and talk about their feelings. The distinction between competitiveness and cooperation has relevance for analysing how the girls in this study operationalised their friendships. I take my understanding of 'cooperative talk' or conversation from Coates (1988, p. 118) as speakers working out a joint point of view which takes precedence over individual assertions and often includes mutual disclosure. Intimacy, as noted earlier, is a strong feature of female talk happening between friends (Reis and Shaver, 1988). For some women intimacy and confiding involves admitting dependence, sharing problems and being emotionally vulnerable. For the girls in this study, who they confided in changed as they grew older. When they were at primary school, most of the girls named their mothers as the first person they would turn to for help solving problems. When they moved onto secondary school they cited their friends as their intimate confidant. However, as is shown in Chapter 4, this was not necessarily the friend they were closest to in terms of the group's hierarchical structure, but usually the girl in the group who had been assigned or taken on the role of the listener. The role of 'the listener' was critical to the functioning of the friendship group, the role and function of the listener is explored in further detail in Chapter 4. The role of talk in how the girls understood, experienced and reflected on their friendships is examined in depth in Chapters 4 and 5.

THE SHIFTING POSITIONS DISCOURSE

Mauthner (2002) describes how the shifting positions discourse enables a capturing of the moment when roles change and power relationships get disrupted, and thereby exposes the post-structural notion of power as 'fluctuating' rather than 'fixed'. Mauthner's study of the shifting positions of the sister ties resulting from changing contexts, for example, marriage, a new job, house purchase or motherhood, has resonance for my study. The differing power positions of the girls in my research, which were seemingly constant within the primary school classroom, were challenged and altered on transferring to secondary school. The point of transfer marked a turning point in the girls' relationships and the positions they occupied within their friendship group at primary school. For Isobel, the group leader at primary school, her shift in position in relation to Hafsha left her vulnerable and to some extent on the margins of the newly formed friendship network. For Shumi, her desire to identify as a black African-Caribbean girl at secondary school was more important to her than maintaining her friendship group from primary school, and for Nila, she no longer took on the role of the 'listener'. What these shifts in positions exemplify is the different locations of power that the girls are placed in as well as adopt and in the process the sense the girls have of their own subjectivity and agency. (Chapters 4, 6 and 7 describe the impact of school transfer on the girls' friendship networks). As Epstein observes:

> *We may occupy positions within different and contradictory discourses being at one and the same time, in positions of relative power and relative powerlessness.....power is not always wielded through coercion, but often through discursive practices which people, as active agents within these practices, either consent to or resist.*(Epstein, 1993, p. 13)

Within this study, the exploration of the discursive positioning of the individual girls as powerful or powerless has not only facilitated a critical understanding of the meaning of 'friendship', but also drawn attention to the dilemma's facing pre adolescent girls in trying to be good and selfless to each other whilst at the same time respond to the current discourse of girls and school success. The conventional and affirmed forms of femininity are now being conflated with masculine aspirations, which are characterised by individualism and autonomy.

Alcoff's notion of subjectivity as positionality enables an engagement with the idea that women 'occupy a range of social and cultural positions simultaneously' (Kenway et al., 1994, p. 199). It implies that women can position themselves and be positioned in different ways in a number of contexts and relationships and even within the same relationship. I illustrate in Chapter 5 how this happens for Hafsha and Shumi, two girls in this study who are 'best friends' out of school, sharing an interest in music and clothes, but have a different relationship to each other in school because of how they are positioned, or position themselves, in relationship to Isobel, the group leader.

I will also illustrate from my data in Chapters 4 and 5, the range of subject positions the girls occupied at different times and in different contexts in their relationship with each other. The work of Walkerdine (1994, 1990) and Hey (1997), whose exploration of girls experiences in school and on the margins of school, sheds light on the girls' multiple and fragmented positions in and outside the classroom. Their work resonates clearly with this study, which documents the ways to which the discursive practices which variously positioned the girls as powerful and powerless was critical to the functioning of the friendship group and to its stability.

CONCLUSION

In this Chapter, I have outlined the theoretical approaches I have adopted for understanding how the girls in this study came to know and understand friendship. I have combined elements of feminist post-structuralism and 'relational psychology', for it seemed to me that both these approaches afforded ways for thinking about how the girls in the study developed accounts of themselves as friends and their relationships to each other. These approaches also assisted in developing an understanding of how the regulatory practices of the girls' teachers and their schools had an impact on the operation of the girls' friendship groups.

The relational psychologists helped to illuminate some of the psychological processes that the pre-adolescent girls in the study experience, especially the link between talk and emotional well being or connectedness. The importance of emotional or 'relational work' in terms of the interactions between the girls contributes to a culture with its own rituals, names and, in some instances, private language. The importance of practices and rituals from buying presents to public affirmation of friendship through ceremonial hugs plays a key role in the construction and deconstruction of friendships. The work of the relational psychologist alongside a post-structural interpretation has been useful for mapping changes in the girls' subjectivities at the time of transition from primary school to secondary school. I do, however, recognise the limitations of the relational psychologists work in so far as they suggest a fairly monolithic engagement between the girls and society.

In contrast with relational psychologists' work, feminist post-structuralist analysis of heterosexual feminine subjectivities offer interpretations which are rooted in dominant cultural and social practices, which form the backdrop of girls' and women's lives.

Feminists have brought two elements to post-structuralism and implicitly two shifts in current understandings in feminist theory. First, the move away from viewing women and girls as a unified group, oppressed by a patriarchal system, thus opening up spaces for resistance, struggle and agency. Secondly, the move away from looking at oppression alone and looking at the unevenness of power, particularly the way women and girls 'are variously positioned in specific contexts' (Maynard, 1995, p. 271). By empirically engaging in post-structuralism during this research, my understanding of power as located in multiple sites has developed further and I have moved away from structures to discourses and power, focusing on 'positioning' rather than agency alone. I would argue the concept of 'positionality' is persuasive in this respect, for as Edwards (1993) observes, it reflects many of the contradictory aspects of women's and girls' experiences as subjects in relationships which can be experienced as both liberating and entrenching, and as fluctuating between connectedness and separateness, contributing 'a social and structural dimension to the relational psychologists work' (Mauthner, 2002, p. 45).

NOTES

[1] I use the term 'post-structuralism' rather than ' post-modernism', although the terms are often used interchangeably, to distinguish between the work of post-modern writers such as Lacan, Lyotard and Baudrillard and the post-structuralism of Derrida and Foucault which has been far more influential in feminist theory (Maynard, M. (1995). *Women's History Review,* **4,** 259-281.)

RESEARCHING THE GIRLS

The purpose of this chapter is to describe the process of data production for this study and to introduce the core group of girls who are the focus of this book. The schools the girls attended are also described, demonstrating the diversity of provision found within large urban cities.

There were two phases to the study. In the first phase, data was drawn from interviews with girls in Years 2, 3, 4 and 6 plus their teachers, in three primary schools. All three schools were urban inner city primary schools. Docklands, an infant school with a nursery attached, served a large urban housing estate. The estate was racially and linguistically diverse with a stable population. Kington School, a 3-11 primary school with an on-site nursery, had a very socially mixed intake drawing from both privately and publicly owned housing. The school was also racially and linguistically diverse. Shakespeare School was another 4-11 primary school, where 99% of the school's child population were Syhleti speakers.

From these interviews I chose the group of girls from Year 6 from Kington Primary School, to become the core group of girls for phase two of the research. The reason for my choice was because Kington appeared to have a genuine interest in the study and some appreciation of the complexity that girls faced when negotiating their friendship groups.

The second phase of the study began a year later and continued for a further three years. The core group of girls were interviewed around the general theme of friendship, but also about their hopes, aspirations and anxieties in relationship to transferring to secondary school. I followed the girls through into their secondary schools and I found myself having to gain access to 6 different secondary schools. The dilemmas of negotiating access within a school are well documented. Sara Delamont reminds us that negotiating access is continuous: 'it is a process, not a simple decision' (Delamont, 1992, p. 8). Gaining and maintaining access to the secondary schools were constant issues throughout the study. Of the 6 schools the girls transferred to, the two mixed schools initially made access to the girls very difficult and then ultimately impossible. It is interesting to note that it was the two co-educational schools which chose not to co-operate, for in addition to the problems that arise in any research project, I would suggest that, perhaps, because girls were the focus of the research, it was accorded with low status by the schools, resulting in loss of access to the girls.

As with phase one, the data in phase two were gathered through interview. The interviews took place during the autumn term and end of Year 6, the beginning and end of Year 7 and the beginning and end of Year 8. The girls were also asked to keep a journal whilst they were in Year 8.

I interviewed Kevin, the girls' class teacher in Year 6, and attempted to interview the girls' form teachers at the end of Year 7. I also interviewed the girls' mothers and two of the girls' fathers in their own homes.

In addition to the core group of girls, I found myself working with two other groups of girls who had heard about the study and wanted to be involved. Indeed, one of their mothers even telephoned me at work requesting that her daughter became part of the study. I did research these girls although in a 'less systematic (and more opportunistic way)' (Hey, 1997, p. 42). I felt these groups of girls could provide a kind of test bed for the themes and patterns that were emerging from the core group of girls.

TALKING TO THE GIRLS -THE INTERVIEW

The primary source of data collection was through semi-structured interviewing, 50 audio taped interviews were conducted with the girls, their teachers and their mothers; in two cases fathers were present. In choosing to interview the girls, I intended to access their ideas, thoughts and memories using their own words to recall and describe their experiences and relationships (Reinharz, 1992). There were four questions which steered the study, and charted the way that friendships are socially constructed, experienced and understood were:

- How do girls understand friendship and to what extent does their understanding shift and alter at the point of transfer to secondary school?
- How far do generally held conceptions of popularity and leadership resonate with the experiences of the girls in the study?
- To what extent do girls resist and subvert dominant discourses of femininity to create their own cultural space and how far is such is resistance 'raced'?
- And can bullying and friendship coexist?

The relationship I had with the girls in the study was a critical factor in the generating of empirical data and I was concerned to make my encounters with the girls as authentic and ethical as possible. In order to explore how the girls negotiated their locations and positioning within their friendship circles, I knew I had to allow them to speak for themselves. I had to build up a level of trust that would facilitate open dialogue. In so far as this was a longitudinal study, I had anticipated there was time over the four years for such trust to develop. However, two of the most critical aspects of the whole research process have been, firstly, my position within it and how this shaped what I did and, secondly, an acknowledgement of the specific issues of power within the research process and in particular around a child's social location, as somebody positioned in relation to that of an adult

I recognised the importance of developing a relationship with the girls, which was built on mutual trust and intimacy from the very beginning of the research process. To achieve this, not only did I self disclose, for example I exchanged personal details about my friends and my relationships with them, I expressed empathy and concern with the girl's dilemmas and acknowledged commonalities with them. I also tried to be sensitive and not probe at particular times during the interview if I felt it would cause distress. The extract below, where Tiffany is talking about bullying amongst her group of friends, provides an example of this.

RG: *Do you think having friends stops people bullying you?*

Tiffany: *It depends on the kind of friends you have, because like when you have friends and people want to bully you they, like, well, they tend to like it if you are getting bullied by someone sometimes.*

Jane: *No! They say 'excuse me, what are you doing?'*

RG: *So was it your friends who were bullying you? Did you do what the people who were bullying you told you to do?*

Jane: *Umm, no.*

Chloe: *Not really.*

RG: *And Tiffany what about you?*

Tiffany: *I forget the question.*

Here Tiffany, by saying she forgets the question, suggested to me that she was uncomfortable with the way the dialogue was progressing and wanted to close the conversation down. (Tiffany's response is discussed in greater detail in Chapter 4).

The extent to which the girls in my study ever felt free of the power relationship that exists between themselves as pre-adolescents and myself as an adult is hard to discern, but like Valerie Hey, I was acutely aware of my own position as a white woman academic whose 'agenda was in part to appropriate parts of their lives for my own use' (Hey, 1997, p. 49).

Although my interviews were semi structured, they also developed conversations and themes picked up on from previous interviews. I attempted to follow where the girls led, so any questions I had were used as starting points and, by using a series of interviews with the same girls, allowed their voices to emerge over time and space. I recognised within the research process that there were multiple inequalities between the girls and myself, which included not only that of researcher and researched, but also adult and child. In an attempt to provide the girls with greater support, alongside interviewing them individually, I also interviewed them with their groups of friends. I asked them to keep journals and the intimate thoughts that were revealed in the journal accounts suggest that some of the girls had developed a great deal of trust in me and my promise of confidentiality. However, within the research process I was constantly struggling with the re-emerging obstacles that come with the authority of age. I never quite achieved putting these and other differences aside and, as a result, I had a sense that some things were always just out of reach, leading to potential misunderstandings and misinterpretation. This tension was something I never felt that I resolved.

There were problems inherent in some of the interviews; initially the question/listening format that operated in school seemed to transfer to the individual interviews, especially in the earlier interviews. I felt at times the girls were searching for the 'right' answers. Davies (1982) expressed similar concerns in her study of conversations she had with 10 and 11 year old children. She found that the children were:

> *putting aside [their] own knowledge derived from experience within the culture of childhood and attempting to tap into the relevant adult knowledge.* (Davies, 1982, p. 33).

Davies emphasises the importance of recognising when children are trying to please the teacher by giving her what she wants and sees these as 'failed interviews'. The problem was perhaps even more complicated for this study in that social constructions of girls' friendship, which are reinforced by literature and the media, made it difficult within the interview process to separate when the girls were trying to please me, please each other, or respond to an idealised notion of friendship (Chapter 4 discusses this issue in detail). However, like Davies respondents, these girls were immensely interested in the research and were keen to participate and, over time, I sensed our relationship became more open, more relaxed, with the girls wanting to make sure I 'got it right'.

THE INTERVIEW IN PRACTICE

I hoped that the girls' stories arising from the interviews would provide some insights into the organisation of 'friendship' groups and the role they play in defining the quality and nature of girls' relationships and their social networks at school. The interviews explored how friendships impact on the girls and their views of 'self' as people, as learners and on their school persona. I also began to make sense of the factors which influenced the rules which govern groups, the makeup of the groups, e.g. size of groups and length of membership, and the group hierarchies. Further, I was able to examine how the complex social processes that characterise such hierarchies affected the performance, both socially and academically, of group members within the classroom. I had intended to supplement the interview data with evidence drawn from detailed playground observations, but found this proved to be counter-productive because the research groups noticed and responded to my presence. However, the girls did keep a journal where I asked them to record their thoughts about friendship and any significant events that had taken place during the day. My intention was to interview all the girls in their named friendship groups, but in some cases I decided against this, as issues about other girls that arose during individual interviews suggested that a group interview might prove too painful to some of the children and possibly provide an opportunity to ostracise individuals within the class. Interviews with class teachers were undertaken and these elicited very different perspectives on the nature of the friendship groups in their classes from those of the girls.

The interviews with parents proved to be difficult. The parents were all very proud of their daughters and were reluctant to offer any insights to potential problems the girls had with their friendships. Each parent insisted that his or her daughter would stand up to a bully and furthermore befriend a girl who found herself in the margins of the classroom. I had hoped my interviews with parents would provide a greater depth of data, which would assist me in making sense of how the girls negotiated their friendships, but the girls' parents tended to want to portray their daughters in a positive light. In a sense, the girls parents are caught up in the same discourse as found in their daughter's narratives, for they too romanticised girls' friendships.

THE JOURNAL

All the girls in the core group were asked to keep a journal of reflections on their friendships. The use of student diaries or journals is well known within feminist pedagogical approaches (Magezis, 1996; Maher and Tetreault, 1994). I encouraged the girls to use the journals in a reflexive way and only to write in them when they felt they had something to say. The keeping of the journals was useful in gaining insight to the 'ever changing experience of being in a friendship group at a particular moment in time and space'. The girls, of course, may well have constructed their journals with me in mind, their imaginary (and real) mode of address (Ellsworth, 1997). Their writing became a personal reflection, yet was also created for the public realm as part of the research project. The girls were aware I was using their journal as part of the research project and responded with varying amounts of detail and disclosure. Shumi was very expansive in her journals, documenting personal 'troubles' which reflects the 'truth telling' so important to her understanding of friendship (see Chapter 7). Whereas Heidi, it could be argued, was starting from a different position, it may be, as the daughter of a lesbian, she was reluctant to disclose anything very much. Nevertheless, most of the girls seemed to enjoy the process of keeping the journal, however, I was aware that they were writing for me and despite telling them otherwise, they viewed the keeping of the journals as a requirement. This pointed further to the unequal power relationship between myself, as the adult researcher, and the girls, who are regulated through the school. It also: 'reveals the impossibility of completely stepping outside dominant practices and positions and the ways that we are continually reconstituted through these' (Burke, 2001, p. 90).

ETHICAL CONCERNS

I found working with the girls in this study challenging and interesting and was conscious that issues of privacy and confidentiality were especially important if the girls were to give complete answers.

Walsker (1991) warns against adult researchers suggesting that their major bias is in seeing children as 'unfinished, in process, not anywhere yet'. She explains further:

> *In everyday life we adults take for granted that children as a category know less than adults, have less experience, are less serious, and are less important than adults in the ongoing work of everyday life. I suggest that for the word less we as sociologists try substituting the word different and consider the theoretical and methodological implications. What is children's knowledge and in what ways is it like and unlike adults' knowledge? To say that children have different experiences from adults focuses on a researchable topic, whereas the designations more/less clearly ground study in judgment.*
> (Waksler, 1991, p. 63)

My view of the girls was that they were individuals in their own right and that my professional experience as a primary school teacher of many years, as well as having a daughter of a similar age to girls in the study, assisted me in building a trusting and intimate relationship with the girls early on in our relationship. Nonetheless, the differential in power between the girls and myself, as discussed earlier in this Chapter, was an every present tension throughout the research, which I felt I never resolved.

DATA ANALYSIS - WHAT THE GIRLS SAID

Although the girls did not have access to the transcripts immediately after their interview, they did get the opportunity to read them, for, with each successive interview, I took the previous interview transcript along with me and it formed the basis for the ensuing discussion. I talked with the girls about what they had said and how they now felt about what they had said, what had altered and what had changed for them. I talked to them about some of the themes I thought had arisen. I considered it to be important for the girls to have an insight into what I was doing with their data. As I indicated earlier in the Chapter, the girls became more sure and more fluent with each successive interview, and the interview process provided some enjoyable moments to celebrate the positive aspects of their friendships, but also some deeply sad moments when the girls seemed genuinely baffled and upset by the behaviour of their friends.

Themes and insights were often revealed in long narratives and the use of multiple interviews and journal keeping enabled me to cross-check between interviews and journal entries. Themes emerged and I was able to get respondent validation with each successive interview, and I would suggest that the data from the multiple interviews provides a depth which could not have been generated from fewer contact times. I was also able to do some cross-checking between the core group of girls and the two other groups of girls who had requested to be part of the study. Furthermore, I drew on my own autobiography. Many feminists draw on autobiography in making decisions about their research areas. The 'self' as a resource in helping to make sense of others lives enables researchers to link the past with the present and as Reinharz suggests: 'enhance our understanding both by adding layers of information and by using one type of data to validate or refine another' (Reinharz, 1992, p. 197).

I make no attempts to claim any 'truths' arising out of the data but, despite this, I would argue that the perspectives and understandings gained are not without power.

INTRODUCING 'THE GIRLS'

This section introduces the girls, both those in the core group and the main players from the other two groups of girls who took part in the research. Table 1 (p. 48) represents diagrammatically key aspects of the girls' profiles as described below.

The Core Group

Isobel:

Isobel was clearly the leader (see Figure 1, p. 78) of the friendship group at Kington Primary School. She is of mixed heritage; her father is from Hong Kong and her mother from Germany. Both her parents are professional; her father is a banker and her mother a doctor, although not practicing at the time. Isobel is the eldest child, she has a brother two years younger than herself. Her family resides in a large Victorian house in the leafier part of a borough which has its share of economic deprivation. Isobel presented herself as confident and self assured during the first two years of the research, but one year after transferring to a private girls secondary school she became less confident and less sure, despite being voted form captain within her first term at Dunwood Girls. However, by the time Year 8 loomed, Isobel has lost her position as the leader of her newly formed group of friends (Chapter 4 discusses Isobel's shifting positions within her network of

43

friends). Whilst at primary school, Isobel was considered by her class teacher to be as able, if not the most able, of any of the children in the class and she continued to succeed academically in her highly pressurised secondary school. Isobel's parents' view of schooling was that, at the end of the school day and at weekends, she needed time to relax and 'chill out' rather than succumb to the pressure to join the huge variety of clubs and activities that were on offer. Her parents also took the view that any problems she had with her peer relations she had to deal with herself.

Shumi:

Shumi, who would describe herself as black, originating from Jamaica, was a member of the inner circle within her group of friends at Kington Primary School. She lives with her mum and her 'grown up' older brother in a less economically advantaged area of South East London. Shumi's mum had been a health professional and is now an independent consultant whose work was mainly targeted at the public sector. Like all of the rest of the girls in the group, Shumi was academically able and invested in school success. Shumi, after transferring to secondary school, also began to invest heavily in her identity as a black student and had, by the end of Year 7, a new group of friends who were exclusively African-Caribbean. Shumi's new group of friends seemed to threaten the dominant values of the school (see Chapter 7), resulting in Shumi's mother spending several meetings at the school mediating on her daughter's behalf.

Shumi's mother's view of friendship was one which encouraged mediation and was inclusive. She believed that; '*Shumi would always stick up for someone who was being left out or bullied*'.

Hafsha:

Hafsha is of mixed race, her mother is a white western woman and her father from the middle east. Hafsha lives in a small semi detached house with her mother in a less economically advantaged area of south east London. Hafsha is no longer in contact with her father. Hafsha's mother works in the Information Technology business. At primary school, Hafsha was a member of the inner circle but, despite this, she presented herself as uncertain and anxious. Hafsha, like Isobel, also secured a scholarship at the same girls' private school. This seemed to increase Hafsha's anxiety, who became particularly worried about how her friendship with Isobel would survive. However, after transferring to secondary school, she quickly became a powerful member of her class and by the end of the first year had established herself as the group leader amongst her newly formed group of friends, a group which included Isobel. Hafsha's mother reflected on her own experiences of friendship at school and used these to provide Hafsha with a great deal of advice on how to handle problematic situations amongst her friends.

Tan:

Tan's family are from Vietnam. She lives in a small terrace house with her grandmother, father, mother and younger brother. Tan's father works for the civil service. Tan is a very hard working student who avoids confrontation, possibly reflecting her parents' advice which actively discourages conflict. Tan was a member of the outer circle of the group of friends whilst at Kington Primary, but despite this, she is one of the most popular girls within the group (Chapter 5 discusses different ways of understanding popularity and leadership). Tan took on the role of listener within the group (see Chapter 4). At secondary school Tan had a much smaller group of friends who, according to the teacher, were all 'high flyers'. Amongst this group there was no established hierarchy in evidence. Tan tends to see the best in everyone, for example, she was teased by the others girls in the class for being 'a boffin' but didn't interpret their comments as malicious or see any malice in the girls actions. Tan was regarded among her teachers as 'a model pupil'.

Heidi:

In terms of economic capital, Heidi represents the least privileged girl in the sample. She lives in publicly owned property, which fronts onto a busy main road in a very poor part of South-East London. Heidi lives with her mother, a younger sister and two younger brothers. Heidi's mother, who describes herself as an artist, is an 'out' lesbian. Heidi's mother is very concerned that Heidi makes the best of the educational opportunities available and invests a lot in her school success. For example, despite living some miles away, Heidi was sent to Kington school, as her mother viewed this particular school as offering the best opportunities for Heidi and the rest of her children. Heidi's mother also took an active role at the primary school, from supporting reading to making costumes for the school play.

When Heidi transferred to Foresters High, she remained friends with Lauren and initially Shumi. Over the four years of working with the girls, Heidi's appearance changed the least, She kept her long plaits and dressed in an androgynous way. Heidi was constantly fearful of being bullied; this could possibly be because she was worried that her closely guarded secret regarding her mother's sexuality would be revealed.

Lauren:

Within the group of friends at primary school, Lauren was on the periphery of the group. Nevertheless, she appeared to be confident and at ease with herself. After transferring to Foresters High, she became a leader amongst her group of friends. Lauren lives in a semi-detached house in South-East London. Both her parents are white; her mother is an office worker and her stepfather a builder. She has a half sister who is ten years her junior. Lauren's mother is very proud of her daughter, who she views as being very socially skilled and very clever. Lauren has a very positive outlook on life and on her relationships with her friends. In her interviews she demonstrated a sophisticated understanding of friendship (see Chapter 4). She is musical and is keen to be part of school productions and other events and activities.

Leila:

Leila is Nigerian and currently lives in one of the poorer parts of South London. Her mother brought her and her younger brother to England when Leila was six years old. Janice, Leila's mother, is a single parent, and had been educated in this country before moving to Nigeria at the age of eight. Janice does not have a regular job but rather through networks in Nigeria she runs several small businesses. Janice invests everything in her children's education and Leila is perceived by her teachers and friends to be 'very bright'. Leila appears to be comfortable on the margins of her group of friends, she is however popular and never excluded from the group. Leila is highly invested in her academic success. Leila was on the periphery of her group whilst at primary school but became an equal member amongst her new group of friends at Park Avenue where no friendship hierarchy was in evidence.

Lisa:

Lisa is of mixed race. Her mother is Jamaican and her father originates from Wales. She has twin sisters who are six years younger than herself. Her parents are buying their property, which is situated in an area of mixed social housing and very close to Kington School. Lisa was a member of the inner circle at primary school but became a leader amongst a new group of friends once she transferred to Askey's Cross. Lisa attended nursery school for a short period, however, for the first three years of her 'formal' schooling Lisa was educated at home by her mother, but after the twins were born she was enrolled at Kington Primary. Her mother is now a childminder and her father writes for a local newspaper. Lisa's mother has most of her relatives living in London and her family spend a great deal of their leisure time with them. Their view of friendship, and one they think Lisa shares, is interesting. They believe that your friends are your family and that any friends made at school are superficial. Lisa's journal entries, however, suggest that, like the other girls in the group, she places a great deal of emotional investment in her friends.

The Other Girls

Melody:

Melody's mother is Eastern European and her father English. She has one sister who is three years older than herself. Of all the girls in the study, Melody is the most economically advantaged, she lives in a huge detached house in a sought after residential area of south London. Melody's mother does not work in paid employment, but is involved in charity work. Her father is an actuary for a large and well known accountancy firm and spends a great deal of time away from the home working and travelling abroad. At primary school, Melody was a powerful leader amongst her group of friends, but after transferring to her secondary school, she lost this position and seemingly drifted from one group of friends to another. Melody was the only girl in the sample to have a sibling in the secondary school she was transferring to.

Sian:

Sian's parents are both white, her father originated from South London and her mother's family are from Southern Ireland. Sian's parents both work full time, her father has his own computer business and her mother is a teacher.
She lives in an old Victorian house in South London. Sian is an only child. At primary school Sian was a member of the inner circle but, after transferring to her secondary school, she made a new set of friends where there was no hierarchy in evidence.

Nila:

Nila is a mixed race girl, her mother is Asian and her father is white British. Both Nila's parents work, her father is the director of Information Technology in a small company and her mother is a teacher. The family live in a semi-detached property in a North London suburb. Nila is an only child who is exceptionally musical. At primary school she was a member of the inner circle although was often pushed out to the periphery of the group. After transferring to high school Nila made friends with a new group of girls and again found herself frequently moving between the inner circle and the periphery of the group. In both her primary and secondary schools Nila found herself positioned as the 'listener' amongst her group of friends.

Carol:

Both Carol's parents are South African. She has a sister who is three years older then herself. Her mother works part time in a private nursery and her father works in the Information Technology field. The family live in a privately owned semi-detached house in North London. At primary school Carol was the leader amongst her group of friends, but after transferring to her secondary school her position became more vulnerable, as her former friends from primary school formed new alliances.

Table 1 - Characteristic of Core Group

Name	Isobel	Shumi	Hafsha	Leila	Tan	Heidi	Lauren	Lisa
Ethnicity – Mother	German	Jamaican *	British *	Nigerian *	Vietnamese	British *	British	Jamaican
Ethnicity – Father	Chinese	Jamaican	Arabic	Nigerian	Vietnamese	-	British	Welsh
Siblings	1 younger brother	1 older brother	Only child	1 younger brother	1 older brother	2 older brothers 1 younger brother	1 younger sister	Younger twin sisters
Secondary School	Private	State	Private	State	State (selective)	State	State	State
Position in Group. Hierarchy at Primary School	Leader	Inner Circle	Inner Circle	Peripheral	Peripheral	Peripheral	Peripheral	Inner Circle
Position in Group. Hierarchy at Secondary School	Peripheral	Inner Circle	Leader	No evident hierarchy	No evident hierarchy	Inner Circle	Leader	Leader

* Single parent

THE SETTINGS

In this section I shall describe the key primary and secondary school where the majority of the research took place.

Kington Primary

Kington Primary is located in a socially and ethically diverse area of southeast London. The immediate surroundings of the school consist of high density housing with a mixture of owner occupied dwellings, both houses and flats, rented accommodation, local authority housing, a refuge and two homes for pupils in care. The school is housed in an old secondary school building and was opened as a primary school only 10 years ago. The four-storey building has the school on the ground floor with the borough's 'Professional Development Centre' upstairs.

When the school was created, the governors were clear that the school should aim for high academic standard; but at the same time embody the broadest definition of education, and be open and welcoming and inclusive of parents, children and the community. The children at Kington call their teachers by their first names and generally had a great deal of respect and affection for them. There is a rich diversity of children from different backgrounds and this difference is 'celebrated' throughout the school year demonstrating how both children and staff value and respect the beliefs of others. The strong equal opportunities policy of the school was underpinned by effective monitoring. Pupils are taught the difference between right and wrong from their earliest days in the school and a strong moral code is implicit throughout the life and work of the school, this is reflected in the relationships that exist between child to child and child and teacher. There are many visitors to the school from the local community, as well as other parts of the world.

The school is vertically grouped and these mixed aged classes are seen as a positive feature of the school by many parents, taking the view that the younger children learn from the good role models of the older children in the class. Whilst this maybe the case, evidence from the study suggests that the Year 6 girls did not socialise with the Year 5 girls who were part of their class and, indeed, viewed them as a nuisance to be tolerated rather than providing any benefit to their class.

The Secondary Schools

Park Avenue Girls School

Park Avenue Girls School is located in an outer – London borough and serves a mixed area, though owner occupied housing is far the most common form of local residence. This state school, which has been awarded specialist school status for

Technology, was, in 1997, identified by Chris Woodhead, the then Chief Inspector for Schools, along with 63 other schools as a school of exceptional quality. In the literature, the Head Teacher defines 'her' school as an 'all-ability' (11-19) school rather than a 'comprehensive', which is its official DfEE designation. Although the school is an 'all girls' school, which calls into question its status as a 'comprehensive' school, I would argue that the pre-fix 'all ability' school is there to draw attention away from its comprehensive status because that is judged to be unappealing to local parents, many of whom may have ambivalent views of the success of the comprehensive system in general. In any event comprehensive schools are formally non-selective, Park Avenue Girls is hardly that. It is an extremely popular and oversubscribed school and in order to gain a place, a formal test is sat on a Saturday morning in the Autumn Term. The results of these tests allow for the school, following government policy, to admit 15% of its annual intake (i.e. 32 pupils) on the basis of academic ability. That leaves about 130 places unaccounted for. These are allocated on the basis of proximity of home to school 'as measured in a straight line'. How far ability informs this process is difficult to gauge, but two points lead me to suspect that the test results of pupils who are not part of the 15% referred to above played some part. Firstly, Leila, who transferred from Kington primary to Park Avenue school, lives a considerable distance from the school and has to negotiate a difficult return journey from home to school each day. Leila is a very able girl whose work and examination results suggest that she is a 'straight A' student. Secondly, that on entry to the school, the attainment of the pupils is higher than the national average (Ofsted Report, 1999). The head of the school subscribes to the notion of 'effectivity' as constructed in the field of new public management, as described by Mahony and Hextell (1997). She has learnt more about how to run the school from the world of commerce than from the world of education;

> *.... schools should borrow a lot of experience and rules from business. I came in with that attitude. It was the approach to education that I'd adopted in my previous school, and it was resoundingly sneered at here by senior staff ... . They referred to it as the Wandsworth Business Model, as if there was something tacky about trying to apply the principles of good management to a school and I've never understood that .... I like the notion of efficiency. If someone wants an appointment with me and I say two minutes past ten because I've got three minutes at that point then I expect it to be at two minutes past ten .....*

(Jane, Headteacher, Park Avenue Girls School)

The school has become so wrapped up in its commercial concerns that it has cut itself off from the public education system designed to offer opportunity to all. I would argue that its engagement with the public sphere via private interests makes its public espousal of equality of opportunity a sham.

Gaining access to the school for research purposes was unproblematic. I benefited from the fact that the school was interested in becoming a 'Training School' and needed a Higher Education institution to validate their bid. Leila's class teacher, however, was also very interested in the research. She organised the interview schedule and the room where the interviews took place, albeit before the start of the school day, making the whole process problem free.

Foresters High Girls School

Foresters High Girls School, in stark contrast to Park Avenue Girls, is a mixed, multi-ethnic all girls comprehensive school. It is positioned in an inner city area of South London, where some of the city's most sought after and expensive accommodation exists cheek by jowl with some of its most run down areas. The school's intake is socially mixed, with the girls coming from a wide geographical area, including areas of deprivation. There is a wide ethnic mix in the school reflecting the rich diversity of the local area. Last year there were 138 refugee students on roll and there is a much larger proportion than nationally (26.8%) of students for whom English is an additional language. The headteacher is viewed by both parents and girls as supportive and caring, but with a will for the school to succeed. The school has worked hard on its equal opportunities policy and this is implemented very effectively. Inclusiveness is a strength. One of the keys to the school's success is the very good provision for the personal development of students – through tutors and the excellent social and personal development programme. The school uses a positive behaviour management approach, which emphasises the need for students to develop self-discipline.

Gaining access to the girls was not problematic. I spoke to the head of year and then wrote individual letters to the girls. I arranged, through them, convenient times to visit, i.e. outside formal lessons. I also secured an interview with their form tutor. Finding a room for the interviews to take place was more problematic for at Foresters High many rooms are locked during the lunch break, but, after some negotiation, we managed to secure a room. Interestingly, the girls were made responsible for facilitating the whole of the interviewing process, possibly reflecting the school's commitment to social and personal development.

Dunwood Girls School

Dunwood Girls School is the one private school in the sample. It is part of the 'Girls Day School Trust' group of schools. The 'Girls Day School Trust' claim to have been at the forefront of girls' education since the trust was set up in 1887 and offers 'high quality education for girls with intellectual promise, at a very competitive cost'. Bursaries and scholarships are awarded from which both Isobel and Hafsha, the girls in this study, benefited. Dunwood Girls is located in an area where like so many areas of London, the 'rich' and the 'poor' live side by side. The girls come to the school from a wide geographical area of London with some coming from as far away as East Sussex, and reflect a broad ethnic mix. The school is non denominational and girls are admitted irrespective of the religious beliefs. The school, like most independent schools, offers a favourable pupil / teacher ratio.

The aim of the school is to offer a broad education, maintaining a strong academic tradition while at the same time developing the whole person.

> *We expect to see students leaving here........prepared for an independent life and capable of making a contribution to society.* (Deputy Headteacher).

The pastoral system in the school is strong and visitors are very welcome. The entrance to the school is via a plush hotel like lobby and one is struck by friendliness of the school. This area is decorated with artwork and magazines heralding the achievements of the school and the individual girls within it. Access to the girls and provision for interviewing them was organised very efficiently by the school, for example, they constructed schedules for the interviews, each girl knew when and where to come, and a room was also organised where the interview could take place without interruption. This may be because the teachers are possibly less hurried than teachers from the state sector, they also may have greater resources at their disposal. As a researcher, this arrangement was excellent. However, the promotion of independence and autonomy as one of the stated key factors in the girls' education seems somewhat undermined by the organisational arrangements of the school. The school were, however, very interested in the research and saw it as making a possible contribution to their pastoral programme.

Askey's Cross

Askey's Cross is a city technology college which is situated in an area of social and economic disadvantage in terms of class and overcrowding of households. It does, however, draw its students from a broad geographical range across three London boroughs and includes a mix of social backgrounds. Within the schools population, 39% of students are from minority ethnic backgrounds and the proportion of children for whom English is a second language is higher than the national average, but below that found in most London schools. The school is heavily oversubscribed with 10 applications for each place. It has a strict entry policy in order to secure a comprehensive intake, however, when the students start at 11 years old, their attainment level is well above the national average. Although students from a range of 'capabilities' above and below average are admitted, a recent Ofsted[1] (2000) report praised the school for its impressive results in examinations in Year 9 and Year 11, which are well above the average in comparison with other schools who take children from similar social and economic backgrounds, these results 'are very high indeed'. Getting access to the school was fairly problematic. After writing to request an interview with Lisa and her friends, I had to make several follow up telephone calls to secure a convenient time to meet. I then went along to the school to find out that the girls involved hadn't been told of the meeting and indeed the school didn't seem to have any record of the appointment. Eventually we met and, at that time, I also managed to get the agreement of the form tutor to be interviewed at the end of the academic year. Again this took two visits, because the form tutor forgot I was coming. When eventually we did meet, she admitted to not really knowing the girls and that I probably knew them better than she did. This less than productive interview led me to question the extent to which the personal and social concerns of the girls was put on the back burner in the school's drive for excellent exam results.

CONCLUSION

The broadly feminist perspective I adopted in the collection and interpretation of the data was in my view both the most appropriate and the one that I was most comfortable with. Drawing on ethnographic method of multiple interviews, journal keeping and my own autobiography I have been able to analyse the responses of the girls and their teachers, which has helped me in making sense of how the girls in this study experience and understand their friendships. In making my biographical details available (see Chapter 1), I am enhancing the validity of my data to the extent that my biography and involvement in the research process is made known to readers in order that they can consider how my role inevitably shaped and coloured the research venture.

I appreciate that there are limitations to the methods I have employed, for example, the analyses that follow from this Chapter are not representative in an equal fashion of all the girls and teachers with whom I spoke. During the research process, two of the girls as I indicated earlier on in the Chapter, were lost from the sample, and few of the girls' secondary school teachers agreed to be interviewed.

Throughout this account I have paid attention to issues of power and control, which is neither easy nor clear. Working with pre-adolescent girls made it even more important that I had to continually exercise reflexivity in terms of power relations and ethics.

In the next Chapter, I will analyse how girls made sense of their friendships. I will show that there are a range of discourses from which the girls drew and manipulated in negotiating their friendships, whilst seemingly responding to the dominant discourse of caring and selflessness. I further explore how the theme of friendship articulates with 'raced' identities and how it becomes possible to conflate friendship with bullying.

NOTES

[1] Ofsted (Office for Standards in Education). The official body for inspecting schools in the UK.

PART B

DEMOCRACY OR HIERARCHY, RHETORIC OR REALITY

Girls Talking about Friendship

The role of friendship as a reference base for children and pre-adolescents has, in recent times, come to be seen as important as that of the family. Research on friendship[1] suggests that friends are pivotal in engendering a feeling of belonging and a sense of identity. However, the type of friendship that children engage in can be qualitatively different depending on the amount of interaction involved in the friendship and the subsequent amount of intimacy and intensity that takes place. Friendship is neither simple nor universal and research further suggests that children who find difficulty in making friends risk becoming socially marginalized amongst their classmates, both within the classroom and outside in the playground.

Friendship (making friends) in schools is the start of children having to negotiate and deal with others outside the family; many children move away from unconditional love to a complex social setting in which affection, approval, affirmation have to be negotiated. Davies (1982) argues that it is through friends that children construct their own separate culture, which is built on shared meanings not easily discernable to adults. She too suggests that it is only by making friends that children gain access to this culture and this, as Blatchford and Sharpe (1994) observe, 'could explain some of the anguish of rejected and isolated children'. Davies further argues that children's friendships are a delicate balance of sharing, obligation and reciprocity and that adult perceptions of the instability of children's friendships are ill conceived. Rather she suggests that children enter into a complex set of strategies in order to secure friendship, not because of the love of a particular individual, but for the purpose of engaging in the functions[2] of friendship. The evidence from this research would support Davies' findings in so far as the girls in the study did negotiate their way within the hierarchy of their friendship group and at times compromised their sense of right and wrong in order to retain their membership of the group. However, whilst there may be some validity to her contention that adults have a different view of friendship from that of children, I would argue that such a position is unhelpful when attempting to reflect on the positive and negative aspects of children's experiences of friendships; this implies that children's friendships are 'secret gardens' which defy adult scrutiny. Whilst it may be true that analysis of children's friendships needs to take account of children's emotional maturity and social development, it is also true that close examination of children's friendships reveal the pain and the bewilderment, experienced by the girls in this study, which results when they find themselves relegated to the margins of, or excluded from, their friendship group. The girls in this study were more often than not unaware of the reasons for their exclusion and had to 'bide their time' until they were included in the peer group once more.

UNDERSTANDING FRIENDSHIP

Much of the research on children's understandings of friendship emphasises both its functional and its temporal nature. In comparing the responses of the young girls, i.e. those in school Year 2, aged 6/7 years old, with those in Year 6, aged 10/11 years old and then again in Year 8, 13/14 years old, this study at a first reading would support this. For the young girls in Year 2, the meanings they attached to friendship were embedded in concrete terms; Jane said:

Someone to play with.

Chloe thought of friendship as:

Someone who would invite you home for tea.

Whilst Tiffany saw it as:

Someone who would not walk away and say you can't play.

Whilst all three comments may suggest a pragmatic orientation to the purposes of friendship, I would argue that Tiffany's comment also gives an insight to her understanding of the fragility of friendship and its attendant power relations. I would further suggest at this age that it is the lack of the girl's verbal competence rather than any taken for granted assumptions about the conditions of friendship, which limit their ability to articulate a more complex understanding. For the girls aged between 10 and 11 years old, their ideas of friendship would at first reading appear to represent a far more intricate set of social relations than that offered by the younger girls. For Lisa, a good friend was someone:

...you could rely on, who you could trust.

For Shumi friendship was about:

... being there for each other

And for Isobel it was all about:

Loyalty.

Whilst such comments resonate with notions of empathy, they also reflect, not only the functional aspects of friendship, but also the potential instability of the relationship should any of the girls fail to live up to its expectations, thus reflecting Tiffany's concerns about friends who:

.. walk away.

Further analysis of the comments of the Year 6 girls and the Year 2 girls would suggest that the girls are saying the same thing although the language of Year 6 girls is more sophisticated. Thus Lisa's emphasis on:

someone you can rely on, who you could trust

would simply seem a more sophisticated articulation of Tiffany's statement that a friend:

is someone who would not walk away and say you can't play.

The same group of girls when interviewed again at the beginning of school Year 8, when they were between 12 and 13 years old, described their friendships in the following way.

Tan: *em, we hang out with each other and we always do group work with each other. And we go with each other in each other's house, we talk to each other. Confide in each other.*

Whilst Shumi thought that friendship in the secondary school:

... is much better because you have real friends........It's about having fun and sticking by your friends through thick and thin.

Lisa saw that:

... the type of friendship I have has changed. In primary school I was surrounded by people I half liked.......Now I have closer friends I can absolutely trust and who I can be myself with.

Although these pre-adolescent girls' understanding of friendship acknowledged what they saw as a qualitative difference in their friendships from primary to secondary school, they nevertheless continued to express both the functional and emotional aspects of friendship.

Given this, it would therefore seem to me that a simple hierarchical developmental model of friendship based on age cannot be sustained and that there is a blurring of the categories of 'friend'. What I mean by that is; understandings of friendship for any individual child are contingent on their experience of friendship with different people and that the social context the children find themselves in plays a far greater part in shaping their understanding of friendship than does their age. For the girls in this study, with the exception of Lauren, their friendship had developed from meeting early on in their primary school, i.e. in the nursery/kindergarten class.

RG: *Tell me, why are you all friends?*

Hafsha: *I know, cos me and Shumi were together at nursery and Shumi liked someone else so I liked this other person.*

Shumi: *No, no, no. Me and Hafsha have known each other for ages. And those two have known each other for ages. And then these two were best friends for a while and then Lisa and me were best friends for a while. So when Lauren was new...we liked her so we kinda let her into the group.*

That Hafsha and Shumi's friendship had endured and indeed become closer throughout their primary careers, would suggest that the friendship was based on more than just age. The data suggests that other factors, both within and without the school, were influential in maintaining and sustaining this friendship group. Shumi, in talking about her friends at the beginning of Year 6, when she was 10 years old, maintains that:

They're like, they are all kind of like different kinds. They've all got their own set of personality, all different, that is why I like them, but then goes on to say that Hafsha is her best friend because: I've got a lot in common with her. Some of my friends I've known longer, but me and Hafsha have got more in common..........we both like clothes, same music and shopping and food.....we like the same kind of stuff.

The shared interests of music and fashion take the friendship of Hafsha and Shumi beyond the school gates and into another set of cultural experiences. Such cultural experiences would seem to be as critical in maintaining their friendship as what happens in the classroom or playground.

Other friendships grew around informal ties such as mothers knowing and liking each other or helping each other with childcare arrangements. Shumi's mum describes her relationship with Audrey:

I think at Primary school there was a bunch that used to hang together, but I have a very close friend who use to pick her (Shumi) up named Audrey, and she used to have Lisa, who was kind of a forced friend if you get my meaning, because of her mum...........And so they were close and Audrey's got such a nice family.......so it was quite nice for us and I just love Audrey as a person anyway. But I wouldn't say Lisa and Shumi are the best of friends. It was more a convenience thing.'

Whilst it could be argued that any friendships are made from who we happen to meet, the girls here were on friendly terms because it suited the parents.

In reflecting back on Shumi's primary school friendships, Shumi's mother acknowledges that her friendship with Audrey was instrumental in the development of Shumi and Lisa's relationship. Her description suggests that, had the families not been so friendly, then the friendship between the two girls may have been far more casual, as she says: "buddies rather than friends". For these two girls their friendship was contingent on the parents' relationship rather than any functional orientation to friendship and as such placed constraints on Shumi and Lisa's sense of agency in their choice of friends. Interestingly after transferring to secondary school, Lisa and Shumi, both reflected rather negatively on their primary school friendship.

DEMOCRACY OR HIERARCHY: RHETORIC OR REALITY

Friendship held certain shared meanings for the girls, which reflected the socially agreed practices amongst the group, practices that according to their responses in interviews were anchored in a basis of intimacy and trust. Hafsha had friends who were:

... easy to trust. You can tell them your secrets. And they are loyal to you and help you when you're in trouble.

Friendship offered a forum for Hafsha where she maintained that she could share her deepest feelings with her other friends, secure in the knowledge that her secrets would be guarded and kept confidential. However, all the girls in the group gave very similar responses when asked about their friendships with each other. Heidi's friends were kind and nice and can keep secrets. For Isobel, her friends were people you could trust and rely on.

The reasons why the girls offered such similar responses in their interviews is unclear, however, I would like to offer two possible explanations. Firstly, the interview process itself. Davies (1982) suggests that, in the context of communication between teacher and child, the child becomes adept and skilful in figuring out what the teacher wants to hear and then supplying the right answer. Davies then goes on to question how far this practice is reflected in the relationship between the adult researcher and child participants, who may continue to provide what they consider to be correct response. The initial interview I had with the girls in the study may well have suffered from this constraining interaction, presenting to me what they thought I wanted to hear, but I had interviewed the girls at critical points during school Years 6, 7 and 8, in their homes and their schools. I would suggest I developed a positive and free relationship with the girls, evidenced by the confidences that they chose to share with me. I also tried to avoid the orthodox interviewing process with a preset agenda and, in following Brown and Gilligan's (1992) model, attempted to 'move where the girls lead'. With regard to the question of what makes someone a good friend, the girls at all points in the research responded with similar feelings irrespective of whether they were in Year 6 or Year 8, whether they were writing in their journals or talking in front of their parents. This could suggest that rather than the interview process producing these similar responses, that the girls within their peer group had constructed an idealized notion of what a friend should be, employing a vocabulary of legitimation and a shared rhetoric which reflected concepts of caring, support and democracy. However, the data from the interviews with the girls suggest that their relationships whilst being articulated as democratic, were in reality enacted as hierarchical.

IDEALIZING FRIENDSHIP

In the culture of the girls' friendship groups at primary school, there was an emphasis on the construction of intimacy and connection. The girls prioritised care for their relationship to each other over independence and competition. They idealized their friendship group and, through affirming their solidarity to each other, articulated to outsiders an egalitarian ethos. Leila describes how:

> *We kind of sit near each other. We hang round together and have jokes. At lunchtime we save tables for each other and we all play together at playtime...We kind of make it hard for other people to get to know us, we just kind of like close off as a group.'*

James maintains that it is 'through such public performances that children evaluate and acknowledge their friendships with one another: being friends must not only be experienced but seen to be experienced' (James, 1993, p. 215). This performative aspect of friendship may also be evident in the girls' physical contact with each other, which was expressed through the ritualised hugs that were part of their daily routine; a journal entry from Isobel emphasises how such performances maintain both the cohesion and hierarchy within the group:

> *even if they (her group) don't like someone, we keep it in the group and we don't tell the person, we just act normally to them, like we give them hugs in the morning to say hello and still let them hang around with us.*

Processes from both within and without the school could be seen to contribute to these idealised forms of friendship. Certainly the staff at Kington School embedded their practices within a culture of equality and respect for all. The school maintained a public profile where pastoral care was seen to be as important as the academic curriculum.

Outside influences, such as the media, were also seen to influence significantly the girls' view of what friendship should be about. As Sian remembered:

> *I always wanted a best friend, just like Tiffany and Bianca were in Eastenders[3], I wanted to have someone I could trust to always be there for me, who I could share secrets with. So when I met Melody in Year 4 and she was so nice to me, at first anyway, I wanted her to be my best friend so we could be just like Tiffany and Bianca. But after she became my friend she kept leaving me out and other stuff. My mum always said that life wasn't like how it is shown on the television. Well now I've got Chloe and she is the best friend anyone could have, she will never let me down I know.*

For Sian, even though she fails to secure a best friend at her primary school and despite her mother's advice, she is still driven to seek the idealised friendship as portrayed in Eastenders. The reasons Sian cites for wanting a best friend reflects, not only the feelings of all the girls in the study, but also the powerful and persuasive values espoused by the media where for girls, reliance on a friend, on passionate intimacy and care is positioned as far more important than independence, status and hierarchy. Interestingly, despite these cultural understandings of friendship, it was still the leaders of the groups who constructed the code of behaviour, and conformity to their wishes was a prerequisite for membership. Isobel, the leader, demanded:

> *loyalty' and 'trust*

from the group, and as Lisa exclaimed:

> *'what Isobel said went'.*

FROM PRIMARY TO SECONDARY SCHOOL

Of the core group within the study, both Hafsha and Lisa went on to become friendship group leaders in their secondary schools and continued to employ the same language of trust and loyalty reflecting the strength and intimacy, which had characterised their friendship group at primary school. McRobbie (1978), in her study of the friendship of adolescent girls, suggests that it is precisely these qualities that enable girls, and in particular working class girls, to cope with the exigencies of patriarchal power in the labour market and in the domestic sphere. However, from the perspective of this study, I would argue that the girls had internalised from popular culture early on in their primary school what it means to be feminine and what particular aspects of femininity are valued and have currency within the institution of the school.

Carol Gilligan's (1990) work has particular resonance for the way friendships were negotiated by the girls in this study. Gilligan and her colleagues' research of girls' entry into adolescence found that girls experience a tension between the desire for independence and autonomy and a desire for connection. The girls' declarations of loyalty to, and trust in, each other were played out as a public performance of friendship, with the girls producing themselves as 'good' and 'selfless'. As Hafsha exclaims:

> *Me and Gretal are best friends (in school) but she expects me not to like or be nice to Csilla at all. Yet on Friday she was sooo nice to Csilla and acting like they were best friends. I got annoyed at her because she was being a hypocrite by not wanting me to be nice to Csilla but then she could be.*

Here Hafsha, in describing her annoyance at Gretal's rather fraudulent behaviour, also illustrates how Gretal, by positioning herself as good and selfless, places Hafsha and her behaviour as both bad and selfish. Following from Walkerdine's contention that being good and being selfless is an impossible ideal, Gretal's desire to be connected to particular friends meant she had to engage with them in ways which presented a veneer of goodness whilst hiding the 'badness.'

The girls were still as concerned as before about having good friends and their friendship groups continued to construct rules which all had to accept if they wished to be or remain a member of the group. However, some of the girls' newly formed friendship groups were not created on the basis of mutual trust or respect and like their friendship group at primary school, continued to be dominated by a leader exerting her influence over the group.

RG: *Is there anybody who makes decisions, who is like a leader within your group?*

Shumi: *Danielle*

RG: *Why's that?*

Shumi: *Because......she doesn't like to be told about herself and if you say 'Danielle whatever you're doing is wrong' or whatever she goes 'shut up' and she knows she's the leader. And she's quite bossy as well...and she likes to hear about herself a lot and everything.*

RG: *Does it upset you when you fall out with her?*

Shumi: *Yeah, because it's so stupid.*

RG: *What do you do about it?*

Shumi: *Nothing, I just keep out of her way. She can be really spiteful when she's horrible.*

For Shumi, the feeling of being excluded from the group by its leader reflected the same pattern of friendship that had taken place at primary school. It would seem that Shumi would rather accept the pain and misery of being marginalised than confront Danielle's behaviour and risk making her an enemy. It could be argued that it is the fear of long term isolation that informs Shumi's decisions around conflicts, driving her away from direct confrontation. Another possible interpretation of Shumi's behaviour is that her avoidance of conflict by remaining silent or staying out of the way is part of the negotiation process. Shumi knows that eventually Danielle will seek her out; Danielle needs to attend to Shumi or the lack of approval or affirmation of Danielle's behaviour by Shumi, which is manifested by her withdrawal from the group, may become infectious and other members of the group may follow Shumi's lead. Interestingly, by the end of Year 8, Danielle was no longer the leader, or indeed a member, of this particular friendship group.

CHANGING SCHOOLS AND LOSING POWER

As I indicated above, when the girls transferred to their secondary schools, shifts in alliances promoted the emergence of new leaders. Both Lisa and Hafsha became powerful group members in their respective schools, but for Isobel, transferring to secondary school resulted in a loss of status, power and popularity.

This year we've been split up in sciences. The only person out of our group that is in my science class is Gretel. I noticed how nice she is to me then. She doesn't make snide remarks about something I've said or done, like she does when we are with the others.

Isobel, who had been the leader of the group when the girls were at Kington primary school and was voted as the form captain within her first term at Dunwood Girls, had, by the time I interviewed her at the beginning of school Year 8, become one of the marginalised girls within her friendship group. Isobel was now subject to Gretal's name calling, whispering and teasing. Isobel may have lost her locus of power due to the different structural and cultural arrangements of the secondary school. For unlike the primary school, where the children are trapped into a particular classroom and have to spend everyday with the same classmates, thus restricting opportunities for meeting and socialising with other children in school, in the secondary school the girls' friendship could only develop in the times, which were few and far between, when they were allowed to congregate with their friendship group outside of lesson time. As the school day was organised into age cohorts, there were no opportunities for meeting up with either younger or older girls, but even within their age cohort, as Amit-Talai found in her research on friendship:

'School interaction was....tightly compressed by the strictures of the school day and a constant subtext of adult apprehensions. So long as the staff remained on school property, they were subject to supervision. Staff monitored the halls, bathrooms, cafeteria and school grounds during recess and lunch time, as well as during class periodicals, a monitoring edge with an undertone of anticipating suspicion. Lunchtime presented an ongoing determination of students to cluster and the equal determination of staff to disperse them. Pupils were not allowed to linger too long in the cafeteria. Once they had finished eating it did not take much time for the teacher to hasten them out...'
(Talai, 1995, p. 151-2, cited in James et al., 1998).

Amit-Talai argues that despite the demands on the time and space by the school and the home at secondary school, friendship groups do emerge. However, she also acknowledges that although such a narrow age setting could foster peer relations rather than inhibit them, she suggests that because of the limited time available there is less time for disclosure and that social intimacies are difficult to maintain.

Certainly Shumi's experience of networking with her friends would support Amit-Talai's research:

Nadine don't really have time to chat because we're not really in the same lessons at school and at lunchtimes she gets tuck lunch and I get school dinners and by the time I get back from school dinners, lunch is nearly over. We can't chat on the phone after school because I don't get time to ring her because of homework and I go out as well. (Shumi)

For Isobel, the loss of access to the intense social relations, which were part of the primary school culture, may have meant a loss of influence over her friendship group.

I talked to Tilly when we were waiting for the teacher to come for Spanish. I asked her why she didn't want to talk to me. She said I always chose such public places to talk about things. (Isobel)

For Isobel, having to discuss publicly the intimate details of a friendship gone wrong, alongside the greater diversity of spaces available for other friendships to develop, may have limited the opportunity for her to influence individual friends, resulting in a loss of authority within the group and a subsequent loss of power. What this suggests is that particular social arrangements and settings make particular 'presentations of self' possible and appropriate, and make what it is to be popular, variable and changeable. As Hafsha explained:

Hafsha: *Well, I think the people in our group, I think they find her (Isobel) quite annoying and she used to be like really popular.*

> *And she's not popular anymore. So I think that's why she keeps coming to me and saying ' Hafsha am I still your best friend?' because she doesn't want to lose me as her friend, so she's kind of not close friends like she believes.*

RG: *Why do you think she's not as popular anymore?*

Hafsha: *I don't really know what changed or what's made a difference...people say they find her annoying now, before you wouldn't get into an argument with her because she always knew what to say, she would always win...but people don't discuss their problems openly in the group they just usually tell them to one person.*

Hafsha's observations of Isobel's loss of popularity lend support to the view that by not having regular and intimate access to the larger group of friends, Isobel was unable to employ her well developed social skills to manipulate and manage the group membership. Nor was she able to influence enough individuals to create the unquestioning following she had enjoyed at primary school.

The girls' reflections on their experience of their primary school friendship could also offer another possible explanation for Isobel's loss of power and possibly a more plausible one. Lisa maintained that:

> *The type of friendship I have has changed. In primary school I was surrounded by people I half liked but I couldn't let go because they were always there bitching about you behind your back. Now I have closer friends who I can absolutely trust and who I can be myself with.*

It would seem that at primary school Lisa had been sucked into a relationship with the group she found almost impossible to leave. She was then able to transfer to secondary school knowing what the pitfalls may be when making new friends and entering into new relationships. Isobel, on the other hand, at the end of her primary years had had no need to reflect about her pattern of friendship, for Isobel her interactions with her friends had been relatively trouble free. The girls' on the periphery had possibly gained a greater understanding of how power operated within their friendship group and this enabled them to observe and assess group dynamics before forming new alliances in Year 7; they were more reflexive about friendship and its purposes and therefore more able to be discerning. As Sian said:

> *I could see who the popular group were, the ones making the most noise, I knew I didn't want to be in their group.*

Whilst Nila went as far as asking her mother to intervene in making sure that she would be in a different class from her existing friendship group when she transferred to secondary school.

Isobel was not the only leader to have suffered in this way; Melody and Carol also found themselves pushed to the margins of newly formed networks of friends. Interestingly, both Melody and Carol reconstructed themselves as victims, as Melody's mother observed:

> *Poor Melody, those other girls are just so nasty, do you know while she was waiting for the concert to start, she was just sitting all alone on the steps and not one of her so called friends came over to see what was wrong.*

Carol on the other hand simply stopped talking to her friends. It could be argued that both these girls, by emphasising their isolation from the other girls, could be attempting to manipulate a situation in order to exhort sympathy from adults and regain attention from their respective network of friends. Nevertheless, like Isobel, their possible lack of reflection has left them vulnerable and their positions as leaders very difficult, if not impossible, to maintain within the new social arrangements they find themselves.

ON BEING A LISTENER

Listening was an interesting dimension of the girls' understandings of friendship that emerged during the interviews. When I asked them

RG: *What makes you a good friend?*

Shumi: *I listen.*

Lisa maintained that:

> *People could talk to her and she would always listen.*

Heidi said:

> *I'm a good listener.*

Indeed, all the girls gave very similar responses to this question. Interestingly within the interviews, listening was not a characteristic applied to the more general and public question of why a particular girl was a good friend, but was seemingly an interpersonal attribute enacted in a private space. It would suggest that whilst being loyal and trustworthy could be seen as moral imperatives, listening would not necessarily carry the same conceptual weight. Being a good listener whilst clearly a desirable quality, was not necessarily something that the girls viewed as an issue for the public realm of the school. However, although all the girls claimed to be good listeners, within the friendship groups where individual girls were ascribed particular roles and responsibilities there was usually one girl who was positioned as a good listener. Shumi describes how all her friends:

... are for something different, Hafsha's for when I'm happy, Isobel for when I'm upset, Tan when I want someone to talk to.

Whilst in the group made up of Carol, Nila, Emma, Elisabeth and Emily, it was Nila who was positioned as the 'good listener', both Nila and Tan were peripheral members of their friendship groups, but the girl leader and members of the inner circle chose to talk to them feeling certain that any confidences would be kept. Such actions seem to suggest that the leaders were placing a great deal of trust in Tan and Nila, a quality that these leaders had publicly stated was a critical quality in any close friendship. With such intimate knowledge one could question why these girls on the periphery did not use this knowledge as a tool to elevate themselves to membership of the inner circle. There are several possible responses to such a question. Firstly, that if 'best friends' share confidences and the listener had a 'best friend ' within the group, then the leader's power may be compromised or diminished as the listeners could conceivably share her secrets - which may include confidences between the leader and the listener. The leader therefore is put in a position where they have to work hard to ensure that the girls who are positioned as listeners are not allowed to develop close friendships with anyone else within the group. Another possible explanation could be that a listener who is not closely allied with anyone, is a role required within any group. It is possible that Nila and Tan fitted the bill early in the group's development and were then prevented by the leader and inner circle members from developing close alliances. Within the genesis of the group, the 'listeners', then, can become victims of their own moral code if they happen to be in the 'right place at the right time.' A further explanation could be that the listener role is developed by some of the marginal members of the group as a tactical way of 'getting by' in the group, for as they are not in a position to 'voice up', they can make themselves valued by keeping quiet and listening to others.

THE 'BLEAK SIDE' OF FRIENDSHIP

The rhetoric of caring, trusting and democracy in opposition to the hierarchy and selfishness, referred to earlier, provides the context for exploring the negative side of the girls' friendships. Bjoerkqvist's and Niemela's (1992) unprecedented study of girls aggression, was premised on the idea that when 'aggression for one reason or another cannot be directed (physically or verbally) at its target, the perpetrator has to find other channels'. The researchers found that the girls were not averse to aggression; they just expressed it in a different and more indirect ways than boys, for example, through social exclusion or passing nasty stories about someone behind her back. The researchers understood these forms of aggression as more subtle and less easy to detect by teachers, but noted their effectiveness in the tighter–knit friendship group of girls; exclusion from a group of friends with whom you were previously intimate is probably more effective and devastating than being unpopular in the looser albeit larger networks of boys. Their findings suggest that the cultural rules by which girls relate to each other demand that they engage in non physical aggression and that, far from being 'sweet' and 'good', the researchers described the girls in their study as 'ruthless', aggressive and 'cruel.'

As discussed earlier, Walkerdine (1990) suggests that the internalised version of femininity involves girls being 'good' and 'selfless', an ideal impossible to maintain within any relationship, she goes on to suggest that the only way girls can respond is to project badness from the self onto others. Walkerdine's analysis highlights the contradictions of femininity,

> 'which can be located within the feminine subject in the psychic production and resolution of desire. The implications of these dynamics indicate that girls' relationships to femininity and to each other can be fraught with difficulties' (Kehily, 2002, p. 5-6).

It is this 'badness' that manifests itself in the exclusionary practices operating within the girls' friendship groups. White's (1990) exploration of friendship points to what she describes as the dark side of friendship. This 'dark side' is manifested by power struggles, exclusion and betrayal. It was this exclusion and betrayal by friends that allowed what seems a contradictory position, that of friend and that of bully, to become conflated in the girls' talk about friends.

RG: *Do you think having friends stops people bullying you?*

Tiffany: *It depends on the kind of friends you have, because like when you have friends and people want to bully you they like, well, they tend to like it if you are getting bullied by someone sometimes.*

Jane: *No! They say 'excuse me, what are you doing?'*

RG: *So was it your friends who were bullying you? Did you do what the people who were bullying you told you to do?*

Jane: *Umm, no.*

Chloe: *Not really.*

RG: *And Tiffany what about you?*

Tiffany: *I forget the question.*

Tiffany's experience of her friends, who sometimes like watching her getting bullied or bully her themselves, highlights an uncomfortable and contradictory position between understandings of friendship and understandings of bullying. Jane, the group leader, in glossing over her complicity in the bullying of Tiffany, does at one and the same time present herself as a good friend who challenges such behaviour, but silences Tiffany who conveniently forgets the question rather than reveal more. By revealing more, Tiffany risks the wrath of Jane, the group leader, resulting in her possible exclusion from the friendship group. Moreover, Jane maintains her power over Tiffany by controlling her version of events.

One of the major difficulties about bullying has been about understanding what bullying is and how to distinguish it from other forms of children's misbehaviour. Roland defines bullying as 'long-standing violence, physical or psychological, conducted by an individual or a group and directed against an individual who is not able to defend himself in that actual situation' (Roland, 1989, p. 21). As Hodge (1993, p. 80) points out, 'the disadvantage of this description is its exclusion of short term behaviour, where various incidents may or may not add up to 'long standing violence', but which can be equally painful or traumatic'. Tattum and Herbert's (1990) definition of bullying as, 'the wilful, conscious desire to hurt, threaten or frighten someone', also seems an inadequate description for describing how the girls both perceived and experienced bullying. It is La Fontaine who possibly provides the most useful definition, for she removes the violent orientation of other definitions and, by drawing upon evidence from Childline[4], is able to define teasing as bullying. 'What is often referred to as teasing sometimes appears indifferent to the feelings of the victim; it seems aimed at exciting the admiration or laughter of other children who, by providing an audience for the bully, participate albeit passively in the bullying' (La Fontaine, 1991, p. 12). However, there is a danger in this kind of inclusive defining of bullying, leading to a view that almost every negative interaction that takes place could be perceived as bullying. Lauren's response to bullying in her school illustrates the dangers of such a broad and encompassing definition.

Lauren: *I would always stick up for the person who is being bullied.*

RG: *Is there much of it going on?*

Lauren: *No, only the very odd occasion, and then it's not really bullying, only light bullying, more like teasing.*

RG: *Oh, teasing?*

Lauren: *Yes. There is actually physical bullying, but the emotional bullying it's so small I don't think it hurts them much........I don't think any class has no bullies.*

In this extract Lauren, who maintains that she would always stick up for someone being bullied, also seems to show a fairly sophisticated understanding of how bullying can be both emotional and physical. However she fails to, or chooses not to, see the impact that 'light bullying' may have on 'them', and in doing so 'others' the victim absolving herself of any responsibility for stopping the bullying and ultimately becoming complicit in its practice.

There is a clear link between power and bullying and, within the structure and culture of the school, bullying can occur in seemingly socially acceptable forms, e.g. academic and sporting achievements. The girl leaders in this study displayed their power in several ways; firstly through their academic ability, secondly through the confidence they had in an unquestioning following from their peer group and lastly also from the explicit support and admiration from their teachers they enjoyed. At Kington School, the girls in Year 6 did not speak freely about their conflicts, it was only when interviewing them again at secondary school that they were prepared to discuss how frustrated and disempowered they had felt at primary school. Lisa admitted that at primary school she was:

with people who weren't really my friends. I can express myself with the friends I have now in a way I never could. Now I can do things to my full potential without anyone being jealous. I can say what I feel quite openly, I can tell them things and I know I won't be betrayed.

The negative ways that Lisa remembered her primary school experience was in terms of betrayal caused by people she trusted and who were 'there for her', but it was the dynamics of the friendship group which silenced Lisa's voice and ended up with Lisa blaming herself for staying with friends who victimized her. It could be argued that in retrospect these friendships are dissolved into something else, a set of relationships that were damaging and changing rather than supportive and empowering and that what is experienced as friendship at a particular point in time maybe regarded very differently with hindsight.

HIDDEN FROM VIEW

In Margaret Atwood's novel Cats Eye, Elaine is seated frozen in fear on a windowsill, where she has been forced to remain in silence by her friends as she waits to find out what she has done wrong. Elaine's father enters the room and asks if the girls are enjoying the parade they have been watching:

Cordelia gets down off her windowsill and slides up onto mine, sitting close beside me.

'We're enjoying it extremely thanks you very much,' she says in her voice for adults. My parents think she has beautiful manners. She puts her arm around

me, gives me a little squeeze, a squeeze of complicity, of instruction. Everything will be all right as long as I sit still and say nothing, reveal nothing ..... As soon as my father is out of the room, Cordelia turns to face me 'How could you?' she says. 'How could you be so impolite? You didn't even answer him.' 'You know what this means don't you? I'm afraid you'll have to be punished.'

In Cat's Eye, Cordelia, like many girl bullies, invests as much time and energy in her good - girl image, presenting herself as nice and caring to adults, as she does in the destruction of Elaine's self esteem.

Some girls' bullying is either invisible to adults or not recognised as bullying. This research suggests that some girls retreat behind a surface of sweetness in order to hurt others in secret. They engage in exclusionary tactics and acts which are difficult to detect by their teachers and other adults. In this study, Sian's exclusion by Melody, the leader, from her group of friends was read by the class teacher as a deficiency in Sian, rather than in Melody. Like Cordelia in the quotation above, Melody's charming and engaging persona dupes the teacher into believing that it is Sian who has created the problem "for wanting Melody all to herself".

Within this study, there are several examples of teachers who, wittingly or unwittingly, collude with the powerful members of the friendship group and, in so doing, enhance their status and power further (see Chapter 5)

In a society where the rules for girls deny them access to open conflict, battles take place in silence. The potency of note passing in negotiating power between friendships, as exemplified in Valerie Hey's (1997) study of female friendship, provides a good example of the less visible way girls manage disagreements which enables forms of bullying to take place that are designed to be kept out of the sight of teachers and other adults. This covert and emotional bullying is not just about not getting caught, but looking like you would never mistreat someone in the first place. In the film Cruel Intentions, Kathryn, who presents herself as sweet, thoughtful and kind, finding herself with a problem, she decides to frame another student because:

Everybody loves me and I intend to keep it that way (Simmons, 2002:23).

Within this study, the leader managed to mediate and control the exclusionary practices and covert forms of bullying and, as discussed in the following Chapter, the manipulating of interpersonal relationships by the leader was a way to maintain their central position and to dominate and direct the consensus among the group. For the rest of the girls in the group, being a 'good' schoolgirl and maintaining perfect relationships necessitated the suppression of disagreements and a form of 'self policing' of their feelings (Hey, 1997).

STAYING WITH YOUR 'FRIENDS'

Why the girls remained part of peer groups that caused such pain and frustration is hard to discern. None of the girls could articulate very clearly why they felt compelled to stay connected to their groups.

RG:	*Why do you stay in the group?*
Nila:	*Well, cos you can't – cos if you didn't, I mean .....because then I might join Alison and Clare's (group), but I wouldn't want them to think I'm interfering with them and you know...in the senior school my mum said that she might probably ask for me to be with different people, so it's quite hard, cos I have been with them since nursery.*
RG:	*It's quite difficult to make the break?*
Nila:	*Yeah.*
RG:	*Would you if you could?*
Nila:	*Yeah, but I quite like Carol, but I know that if I'm with Carol, then, if you are with one of them, then I think you have to be with all of them.*

It would seem that Nila does not quite have enough strength to disengage from this powerful network of girls. Nila may consider that the risk of changing friendship groups could lead to a situation where she finds herself betwixt and between groups and friendless and that perhaps the risks of total isolation are too great. It could be that she recognises that status in the classroom is often related to group membership. However, rather than admitting to either of these possibilities, she provides two possible explanations for remaining in the group. Firstly, in recognising that if she left the group she would need other friends, but then maintains that she would not wish to disrupt the friendship group of Alison and Clare. Interestingly, Nila had shared a room with Alison and Clare on a school trip earlier in the year and they had all become good friends. The second explanation Nila offers is her desire to remain friends with Carol, one of the girls in the group, even though she dislikes all of the others. So, rather than place herself in a vulnerable position, Nila's strategy for escape from this rather binding situation is to look to the future and with her mother's support, be placed in a different class from her present friendship group at the point of transferring to high school.

In the case of Sian, her damaged self-esteem had sapped any confidence she may have had to remove herself from a very disempowering relationship to join another group.

If I'm not friends with Melody then Stephanie won't be my friend nor will Pippa and I'll end up with no friends at all.

Sian, by choosing to associate with Melody, chose a damaged relationship over a perception that she would have no relationship with anyone. Such a tough choice highlights how Sian was not prepared to risk either the emotional isolation of not staying within the friendship group led by Melody, nor the social isolation of having no one to sit with, play with or walk home with.

The leaders of the groups tend to be very socially skilled, but it would also seem they have a charismatic and a seductive quality which, as Simmons (2002, p. 62) observes, results in the leaders having an *'almost gravitational pulls on their victims.'* As evidenced by Nila and Sian above, 'the friendship is mesmerizing, and often the victim is gripped by a dual desire to be consumed and released by her friend.

CONCLUSION

This Chapter has illustrated the dilemma that girls face in trying to understand and respond to constructions of friendship idealized by the culture of the school and wider society, alongside a need for recognition of their own power, status and independence. For all the girls in the study, apart from the leaders, being caught between doing what is right for themselves, where they become positioned as self-seeking, or ignoring their own needs for the good of others, becomes part of their everyday relationships with their friends. Within the Chapter an exploration of the ways in which characteristics of friendship are played out and experienced within the context of the school has shown the extent to which understandings and patterns of friendship change between the girls' primary years and their early years of secondary schools. Furthermore by reflecting on the 'negative' side of friendship I have explored the seemingly contradictory position arising out of some of the girls' narratives, that a friend can also be a bully.

This Chapter also highlights the vital importance of the girls' social relationships and their need to belong. Some of the girls in this study avoided being alone at all costs, including remaining in damaged relationships. Their fear of isolation and exclusion was so great that rather than risk finding alternative friends, they clung onto their existing and inadequate friendships, for to find themselves alone was to awful to imagine

NOTES

[1] (Hey, 1997; James, 1993; Davies, 1982)

[2] Deegan (1996), in citing Ginsburg, Gottman and Parker (1986, p.5), finds examples of the functions of friendship in childhood to include 'the positive, promotive influences of general peer interaction on children's current and long term adjustment and maturity'. Indeed, Ginsburg, Gottman and Parker (1986) maintain that within developmental research on children's' friendship and friendship

expectation, there are five functions in evidence; companionship, physical support, ego support/enhancement, social comparison, and intimacy.

[3] Eastenders is a soap opera based on a community living in London's East End.

[4] Childline is a free and confidential 24-hour helpline for children and young people in the UK. Children and young people can call to talk about any problem; counsellors are always there to help.

INCLUSION, EXCLUSION

Breaking the Moral Code

This Chapter concerns itself with issues of stratification, status and power. By focusing on the constitution and nature of the friendship groups, I explore how friendship groups in the primary schools studied, were structured. I also consider questions of leadership through an analysis of common understandings of popularity. What is it that makes some children seemingly popular? How do individuals within the peer group gain status as leaders? How do particular groups become powerful? The Chapter also discusses the complex relations that the girls who form the 'inner circle' (see Figure 1, page 78) of the friendship group have to engage in order to secure their position within the group hierarchy, alongside a consideration of those girls located on the periphery of the friendship group.

Through a detailed analysis of the girls talking about themselves and their friends, it became apparent that the dynamics of their networks of friends were such that the groups were focused around a single leader, with a set of girls forming an 'inner circle' and an additional pool of girls who were on the periphery. The complex, internal dynamics of friendship groups meant that, whilst it was not easy to discern why an individual emerges as a leader, it was possible to ascertain how, once she was positioned, her leadership was sustained and maintained by the discursive practices entered into with other friends in the group and her class teacher. Similarly, developing an understanding of the composition and operation of the 'inner circle' was not a simple process; their relationship to each other and the group leader was not only complex but also sometimes fraught. The inner circle was usually made up of two or three group members who were close to each other and in some cases had more in common than they did with the leader, e.g. Shumi and Hafsha, two 'inner circle' members, were extremely good friends out of school, they enjoyed shopping, liked the same sort of music and had similar taste in clothes. The outer circle or periphery consisted of girls who tended to have some form of link to one or more of the other girls in the above tier, e.g. Shumi and Lisa were friends because their parents were friends. This peripheral group formed the main bulk of group membership.

FIGURE 1: Structure of Friendship Groups

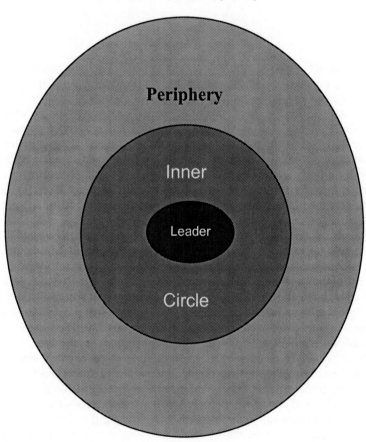

TABLE 2: Girls' Friendship Groups in Primary School

Docklands		Kington		Shakespeare	
Year 2		**Year 4**		**Year 4**	
Jane	L	Sally	L	Anisha	L
Chloe	**I/C**	**Eve**	**I/C**	**Taheera**	**I/C**
Rachel	**I/C**	**Katie**	**I/C**	**Celine**	**I/C**
Tiffany	**I/C**	**Mandy**	**I/C**	**Mamianna**	**I/C**
Catherine	*P*	*Leila*	*P*	*Leelah*	*P*
Lauren	*P*	*Ellen*	*P*	*Cleo*	*P*
				Bela	*P*

Kington		Sandown		Heathfield	
Year 6		**Year 6**		**Year 6**	
Isobel	L	Melody	L	Carol	L
Hafsha	**I/C**	**Sian**	**I/C**	**Hilary**	**I/C**
Shumi	**I/C**	**Stephanie**	**I/C**	**Emma**	**I/C**
Lisa	**I/C**	*Catherine*	*P*	**Nila**	**I/C**
Tan	*P*	*Pippa*	*P*	*Lucy*	*P*
Lauren	*P*	*Maria*	*P*	*Elisabeth*	*P*
Kate	*P*			*Helen*	*P*
Jean	*P*				
Leila	*P*				
Heidi	*P*				

Key:	L	=	Leader
	I/C	**=**	**Inner Circle**
	P	*=*	*Periphery*

All the girls studied placed a high investment in their friendship group, although generalisations about how membership of the group influenced an individuals' self esteem, confidence and achievement in school, were difficult to make. However an analysis of the data collected from the interviews, questionnaires and their journals revealed key signifiers relating to the management and maintenance of the structure of their close friendship group.

LEADERSHIP

As suggested earlier it was difficult to identify what it was that positioned someone as a leader within their peer group and furthermore what is was that made other members of the group so ready to comply with the leader's wishes and demands. One of the strongest aspects of peer cultures that all children have to wrestle with is the notion of popularity. What makes someone popular or unpopular? Does being popular give automatic status and rank in the group's hierarchal structure? Are leaders always the most popular within their peer group and how popular are these leaders with the rest of the class? A consideration of some of the literature on popularity suggests that girls are valued because of their sociability and attractiveness and that the more powerful girls are the ones who have the ability to establish and manage relationships with others. In her study of popularity amongst adolescent girls, Donna Eder found that popularity had different meanings. She found that, on the whole, popular girls were the ones who were most visible and who everybody knew by name. She also found that one of the main factors that determined visibility was attractiveness. However, whilst many of the girls in her study agreed that popular girls were well liked and considered nice and friendly, other girls described the popular girls as being: 'stuck – up and unfriendly and clearly stated their dislike for them' (Eder, 1985, p. 15). A study by Schofield (1981), who explored complementary and conflicting identities and interactions in a middle school, found that white girls avoided interaction with black girls because they were intimidated by what they perceived as the black girls more aggressive style of talk. However black girls assumed that they were being avoided because the white girls thought they were too good to play or work with them. Schofield argued that because these social images had hindered interactions between the two groups these misunderstandings were never cleared up. Thus, in general, the tendency to interpret all acts of being ignored as one of being 'stuck –up' can hinder the development of positive peer relations amongst girls.

It has been argued that the determinants of popularity are: 'embedded within our idealized models of masculinity and femininity and that both boys and girls: actively synthesize from the larger culture and apply it to themselves and each other' (Adler et al., 1992, p. 170). For the girls in this study, these idealized models of femininity were played out against a more contemporary backdrop of girl's achievement. Within this Chapter, I explore the role of popularity in determining how the girls in their primary schools organised themselves into groups or cliques and how individuals were positioned in the group hierarchy according to relative perceptions of each other as popular or unpopular, and to what extent the readings on popularity had resonance for them.

Some of the most significant signifiers of popularity identified in readings on popularity are family background, socio economic status, academic ability, physical appearance and social awareness leading to inclusionary and exclusionary practices. These different signifiers found different degrees of resonance for the popularity or unpopularity of the girls within this study.

FAMILY BACKGROUND AND ABILITY

Studies of popularity amongst adolescent girls[1] found that the socio economic status of the girls' family background was highly influential. All the girls in this study went to primary schools which had socially and racially mixed intakes, and the makeup of the group from Kington, which included Isobel, Shumi, Lisa, Hafsha, Leila, Jean and Heidi reflected this mix (Chapter 3, provides details of the girls' ethnicity). Isobel, however, the group leader, did seem to have far greater access to privileges associated with middle class families than the other members of the peer group, but the impact this had on her popularity within the class is hard to discern. There was a less visible difference in terms of clothes in that dress codes were regulated through an imposed school uniform (although there was a preoccupation with physical appearance by Shumi and Hafsha, two members of the inner circle), the size and type of housing would have been known amongst the group and the girls would possibly be aware of their friend's parents occupation. For this group, however, at the primary school level, there tended to be a general flattening out of class differences and the relative invisibility of class distinctions, which resulted in the girls from less affluent backgrounds being integrated into the peer group. One possible explanation for this is ability. Ability is frequently cited in research (Quicke and Winter, 1995) as a significant source of popularity and this group of friends, throughout their primary school, had been identified by their teachers and parents as being academically orientated. The girls had worked hard and gained both teacher approval and status from their classmates. As ability grouping tends to increase in the latter years of the primary school, this friendship group had grown closer and gained strength and popularity from their academic performance coupled with explicit endorsement from Kevin, their class teacher:

I mean it's been very positive for that group because they have really, I don't know how to describe it, the fact that they are focused on that academic side of things actually has benefited, you know, everybody..........I also think that it is so good that they then ...they are very vocal and articulate and not dominated by the boys in the class.

with Isobel, the group leader's abilities being particularly celebrated:

She is very, very, very intelligent........clearly outstanding in many respects.

Kevin's response reflected those of other teachers interviewed. All these teachers were sympathetic to the group leaders and clearly liked the girls. This may be because they were viewed as very bright:

Anisha did a piece of really lovely work. I forget to praise Anisha because she is so clever - the usual syndrome, and it was absolutely fantastic and I said it was fantastic and I sent her to Maria, the head teacher, to show it.
(Mary, Year 4 teacher)

Anisha's performance here serves two purposes, not only is Anisha and her work being valorised publicly in the eyes of her classmates by Mary the class teacher, but by being sent to Maria, the head teacher, Anisha's efforts provide Mary with a powerful source for 'legitimating' her own performance as a 'good' and 'effective' teacher to the head of the school. In the friendship group including Carol, Nila and Hilary, the constant affirmation of Carol's abilities by Mrs Knight, the class teacher, became almost ritualised, leading to an uncritical appraisal of her 'true' abilities, e.g. Carol, who is apparently excellent at maths but not so good at English, was one of only two children in the year group asked to sit the level 6 English SAT[2] test, even though their were several other children in the class who had done as well, if not better, on the tests running up to the formal tests. The regular positioning of Carol as so much more able than her peers gave her access to high status amongst her friendship group and, like Mary, the teacher referred to earlier, also confirmed for Mrs Knight her worth as a teacher in the current testing regime operating in English schools. Mary's and Mrs Knight's construction of themselves as successful teachers, resonates strongly with research evidence (Moore et al., 2002), which found that the performance of pupils, as measured through SATs and GCSEs[3], played a significant role in the construction of teacher identity.

PHYSICAL APPEARANCE

Whilst the girls at Kington School put academic performance ahead of physical appearance, research by suggests that a powerful determinant of girls' popularity is their physical attractiveness. They maintain that grooming and appearance are not only major topics of girls' conversations, but a source of popularity. Girls are socialised into these norms of appearance from a very early age. Adler et al (1992) describes how a group of kindergarten girls expressed their upset and disappointment about another girl in their class because they felt that she was popular and they were not.

Jen: *It's just that she has a lot of money but we don't, so its like that's why she has the prettiest clothes and you know the prettiest makeup.*

Liz: *And she thinks like she's the prettiest girl in the whole school. Just because she's blonde and all the boys like her.*

Anita: *And she thinks only she can have Erin [a well liked girl] as her friend and not even us, she doesn't even play with us, and that's not very nice* (Adler et al., 1992, p. 179).

The perception that popularity was determined by physical appearance was fully evidenced by these very young children. These aspects of appearance, such as clothing, hairstyles and attractiveness to boys, were even more salient with some of the older girls. Melody, for example, openly admitted that she liked Rebecca *because she was pretty and therefore attractive to boys.* Whilst Hilary, copying

Carol, the group leader in her friendship group, had her long luxurious hair cut short in an attempt to look older and therefore '*more interesting to boys*'.

In a recent Channel 4 television documentary (March, 2003), Marmie, the leader of the 'cool' gang, was seen to be socializing the rest of her friendship group into the norms of appearance and associated social status. Jade, a not so 'cool' outsider, desperate to gain group membership, was relieved when Marmie, at the behest of Tricia the head teacher, allowed her to join in with the nail painting and hairdressing activities being orchestrated by Marmie. These values and attitudes are part of the heterosexist discourse that seek to shape and fashion girls' future identities from an early age.

That frightens us. Whatever has happened to them, bulging them, softening them, causing them to walk rather than run, as if there's some invisible leash around their necks, holding them in check. Whatever it is, it may happen to us too (Atwood, 1988, p. 93).

SOCIAL AWARENESS – INCLUSION AND EXCLUSION

Indications of a child's popularity is generally understood to be either the child who is the most cited as being liked by the greatest number of peers or, possibly, the child who is the most influential in setting group opinions and setting boundaries for group membership in the classroom. The responses arising out of this study, however, would suggest that no assumptions can be made regarding the naming of children as friends and their subsequent popularity, but it does acknowledge that the seemingly most popular girls are able to control and manipulate their peer group. Within this study, the leaders in all of the groups demonstrated a high degree of sophistication in their social and interpersonal skills. They used their social skills to establish friendship with peers and adults alike. They gave support, constructive criticism and were able, if they chose, to make not only their peers but also their teachers feel comfortable in their presence. Their maturity and mental adroitness enabled them to 'read' situations and turn them to their advantage. However, in constructing and maintaining their popularity they often were manipulative, domineering and ultimately controlling.

As Sian, a Year 6 girl, reveals whenever she is asked to name a friend, she: *always chooses Melody, 'cos if I didn't and she found out she wouldn't speak to me and then neither would Stephanie or Pippa*, and when pressed by the question *If you knew that Melody wouldn't find out, who would you choose then?* Sian replied: *Maria probably.*

Sian's reasons for choosing Melody challenge the assumption that the girl who is chosen most often as a friend by the peer group is the most popular. What the extract suggests is that Melody has established a locus of control where she is able to manipulate others in the group, i.e. Stephanie and Pippa, to establish and maintain her central position. Her power comes from being confident in the support she receives from group members and this gives her the freedom to make life difficult for members like Sian, who are part of her own clique. Nila's observation gives further recognition to this process:

I think it is not always the most popular one who is the leader, it's the one who people are, like, frightened of and the ones who have power over the group, like, why they think that if they are not friends with that person, they will drift away, apart from the group. (Nila)

Nila's comments provide evidence that she can clearly differentiate between popularity and the status enjoyed by the group leader and that it is, once again, the fear of exclusion which plays a major part in keeping the leader in their place in the hierarchy.

Similar complexities were revealed when the girls in the study were asked to name their best friend in each of the groups studied. The narratives relating to the importance of having a 'best friend' were remarkably similar and contingent upon an individual's position within the group hierarchy. The leaders within the groups were consistently chosen by the other members as a friend or best friend and frequently identified as the person the inner circle would most *like* to have as a 'best friend'. This was true even when the leaders had little or no time for the person choosing. Furthermore, when the dominant members of the group were asked about their best friend, their responses proved to be measured. For example, amongst the younger girls, it was noticeable that the leaders of each of the groups appeared to be uncertain about exactly who their *best* friend was. In the Year 2 friendship group, which included Jane, Chloe, Rachel and Tiffany, Jane was asked about best friends and she appeared to have reservations about identifying her best friend:

Probably Tiffany, maybe, because er, 'cos, Chloe, er, normally er, she, she does bully me sometimes but it's only if she is, um, in the mood for, like not playing. Um, if she's not in the mood for playing she's a bit bullyish but apart from that she's nice to everyone. So Tiffany's my best friend. (Jane)

When Jane was also asked to speculate on whether she was Tiffany's, Chloe's or someone else's best friend, she did not mention Chloe and confidently replied:

I'm Tiffany's... 'Cos she said so yesterday and she pleaded with her mum to let me go and play.

And then added:

I'm probably Rachel's best friend. She thinks I'm her best friend but I don't really like Rachel that much 'cos she bullies me sometimes. I don't really like Rachel ...

It is interesting to note that Jane's reference to bullying[4] by two other members of the inner circle provides her with a form of legitimacy for the exclusionary practices she engages with. Jane also seems to be aware of the possible lack of reciprocity for being someone's best friend.

The pattern of uncertainty about the leader's choice of best friend was repeated amongst the Year 4 and Year 6 friendship groups. Sally (Year 4), for example, volunteered the following:

...I've got lots of friends and they all, I don't know, but they all want to be with me.

Whilst Eve (Year 4) was in no doubt that Sally was her best friend, Sally, the group's leader, did not confirm this, choosing instead to hesitate and appear undecided:

Well, I don't really know. I suppose Eve, but Mandy and Katie are my best friends.

However when Sally was asked who Eve would say was her best friend, Sally, with no hesitation, answered: *Definitely me.*

Whilst it is possible that the leaders of the groups, in trying to maintain a following, may have found it more difficult than the inner circle to identify a best friend, these extracts do seem to suggest, however, that the leaders within the groups had the luxury of being able to pick and choose their best friends as it pleased them. Also, the picture that these conversations paint seems to confirm the view that girls' friendship patterns are both fluid and dynamic (Nilan, 1991). This may be so for the girls in the 'inner circle' but for Sally, Isobel, Jane, Melody, Carol and Anisha, the leaders in each of the groups, this is not the case. Their positions are seemingly stable and secure at the top of the hierarchy. This security arises from the high self-esteem they enjoy, knowing that the other girls want to be their friends and, in fact, will vie with each other for the privilege. A number of Anisha's comments revealed that she was not unaware of either her secure position or the competition for her favours:

If I be someone else's partner she [Celine] says I'm not your friend, but at the end she makes up. (Anisha)

INCLUSION AND EXCLUSION

The leaders in each of the groups had the ability to express themselves in a mature manner, to read the inter and intra group dynamics, manage and organise others and set attitudes for others to follow, resulting in their dominance of their friendship group. Furthermore, in their desire to be popular, they engaged in both inclusionary and exclusionary practices with both their peer group and other classmates. The consequences for a girl in this situation are brilliantly portrayed in Margaret Atwood's novel Cat's Eye (1988).

> *Carol is in my classroom, and it's her job to report to Cordelia what I do and say all day.........They comment on the kind of lunch I have, how I hold my sandwich, how I chew. On the way home from school I have to walk in front of them, or behind. In front is worse because they talk about how I'm walking, how I look from behind.........They are my friends, my girlfriends , my best friends.........I'm terrified of loosing them. I want to please.*
> (Atwood, 1988, p. 120).

Margaret Atwood, through the character of Cordelia, illustrates how leaders in friendship groups have the power to set the boundaries for the group, make decisions about membership of the group and raise or lower the status and popularity of individual members of the group through her specific engagement, or indeed lack of it, with individuals.

In this study, there was a significant difference between the organisation and maintenance of the young girls' friendship groups and those composed of the older girls, referred to in Chapter 1, involved in Nilan's (1991) research. Unlike the adolescent girls in Australia, all of whom appeared to be involved in, or cognisant of, the reasons for inclusion or exclusion, not all of the girls in the younger friendship groups in this study were equally involved in the process of deciding who was 'in' and who was 'out'. That this was not a fully democratic process was clear, given that sometimes the children in the 'inner circle' and those on the periphery were not clear about the reasons for the actions of the 'leader' or the rest of the group. Thus, amongst the children in Years 2, 3 and 4, the following sort of comments were relatively common:

> *I'd like to be her friend but she doesn't* (Year 4).

> *She just goes away and says you can't play with her* (Year 4).

Another Year 4 girl said that she and her best friend, who happened to be the group leader, never had an argument, instead she: *just says she's not my friend*. What these comments suggest is that friendship is not so much a quality of a relationship as a form of social exchange or gift which can be bestowed or taken away.

It is possible that the perception of intra-group instability originates from this lack of democracy and resulting lack of clarity about the moral code, which results in the girls within the 'inner circle' never being absolutely certain about all the rules determining membership of the group. With older children, it would appear that the moral code was discussed more explicitly and decisions about who can or cannot 'belong' appeared to be more consensual, although it is interesting to note that one child who was liked by two members of the Year 6 at Kington School was not admitted to the group, possibly because she was already part of another group or possibly because the leader of the group did not like her.

As Isobel, the group leader, exclaimed: *you've got to be loyal to be part of this group, she's not our type..... not loyal.* Loyalty was often highlighted as an important factor in this friendship group, with Isobel claiming that her group were special, with each member of the group contributing to the group's strength and cohesiveness. Interestingly, despite Isobel's perception of the group's modus operandi, the decision to exclude Laura was made by her alone.

In the Year 2/3 group, a similar process of boundary maintenance occurred:

RG: *You know your group, if someone wants to come and join it,*
   do
           you mind? Do you let anybody come?

Chloe: *Yeah.*

Jane: *It depends. If it's like R or T [2 boys]*

RG: *But what about other girls?*

Jane: *We don't let Chloe and Therese be friends.*
Chloe: *I don't like her! I don't like her!*
[Year 2/3 group interview]

From the children's responses during the interviews, it would also seem feasible to suggest that the leader within each of the groups generates this insecurity regarding group membership as a strategy to maintain control of the group.

Furthermore, it would seem that these groups are not constructed on the basis of mutual trust, but on the basis of domination as the leader exerts emotional power over the other members of the group. Nevertheless, these girl leaders presented themselves during their interviews as unassuming, modest, reliable and helpful. Their responses were sophisticated and gave explicit acknowledgement to their power, both in relationship to the group and also in their ability to manage the school system. As Anisha told us:

Anisha:	*Sometimes if I tell Taheera I'm Celine's best friend as well, they all get upset.*
RG:	*Who gets upset?*
Anisha:	*All these others, Taheera, Mamianna and Leelah.*

Jane's response also illustrates a degree of patronage towards her friends and furthermore exposes a level of confidence in her teacher who, she believes, will see her as blameless in any disagreeable exchange:

I don't like to get my friends into trouble so if I think my friends will get in trouble I don't tell the teacher.

Anisha, who also doesn't tell the teacher: *because it gets them into big trouble and all*, echoes the same level of confidence in her position.

When the Year 6 girls were asked to name their best friend, Isobel, the group leader, answered: *Probably Hafsha*, but when the group were talking about their move to secondary school, Isobel did not affirm her friendship with Hafsha, despite the fact that both are to go to the same secondary school. Hafsha expressed her anxiety that Isobel may leave her for new friends when they moved to secondary school, and Shumi emphasised that Isobel: *doesn't have to worry [she] gets friends easily*. It was noticeable that Isobel made no effort to reassure Hafsha of the invulnerability of their friendship and, by not doing so, maintained her powerful position within the group.

THE INNER CIRCLE

...different troupes of girls and individual girls within those troupes are respectively empowered, disenfranchised, evaluated.....
(Hey, 1997)

Status and power in the groups was directly related to the social positioning of the individual members. Individuals who were most closely aligned to the leaders were more popular. The hierarchical structure of the group and the shifts in position and relationships within them may have caused friendship loyalties to be less reliable than in other groups not characterised by hierarchical structures.

The positioning of the girls as shown in Table 2, p. 79 merely represents the state of the group at the time of interviewing. It was clear that all the girls in the group, apart from the leader, were anxious about the possibility of being excluded from the group. This anxiety was manifested through the girls' clearly expressed desire 'not to be left out'. This was a recurrent theme in the interviews with the girls, regardless of whether they were six or eleven. When a seven year old, for example, was asked how she would like to change her friends she replied that she would like all her friends to: *be nice all the time and stop leaving me out*. Similarly, a girl in a Year 4 class in a different school said that she wished her friend would: *be my friend for all the time*.

In this respect, this research with young girls does resonate with the research findings of Nilan (1991) who explored the friendships of adolescent girls in Australia. Nilan argued that girls' friendships were not an immutable object but rather 'an on-going process' involving the participants in exploring between themselves what it means to be friends, which is underpinned by developing and sharing a mutually recognised moral order. The children's responses during the interviews highlighted that the children involved in this study, although between three and six years younger than those in Nilan's study, also knew that the composition and internal organisation of the groups was open to change. In addition, it was evident that most understood that adherence to a certain moral code was a necessary part of successful friendships as they mentioned the importance of factors such as kindness, loyalty, mutual support and understanding, and discretion when talking about friends and friendships. When asked what made her a 'good' friend, a Year 2 child replied:

I'm kind to people, nice to people who are upset. And, um, I don't tell secrets.

A Year 6 girl explained that she was a 'good friend' because:

I keep secrets so they can trust me. If someone is left out I usually chat to them and keep them company so they don't feel left out. I'm loyal.

The comments made by the children in this study echoed those made by primary aged children involved in earlier research carried out by Davies twenty five years ago, in 1982. The similarity between the responses of the children separated by almost twenty five years suggests that certain elements of the moral code governing young children's friendships remains fairly constant despite changing contexts.

Membership of the inner circle was indeed dynamic and required active effort to sustain it. The popular members of the inner circle had to put repeated effort into their friendship alignments to maintain their central position relative to the girls just below them. Efforts to protect themselves from the potential incursions of others took several forms. If the leader felt that other members of their group were growing in popularity, instead of either attempting to exclude them from the group or hold them in place, the leader would shift their base of support to less popular group members and in so doing replace the problematic friends with new ones. Alternatively, the leaders would split close friends in the 'inner circle' apart. This happened when Melody began to get the feeling that Sian and Catherine were becoming too popular in the group, she stopped inviting Sian over to her house, excluded her from other activities and talked about her behind her back. Melody then began to play with Catherine and other group members, pushing Sian out and bringing Catherine and others to the fore.

Concomitantly, in an effort to remain as part of the group there was evidence that some of the children were willing to compromise their 'real' feelings. Chloe for example denied her friendship with Therese when covertly challenged by the group's leader, and in so doing had put loyalty to the group above loyalty to an individual outside the group. Similarly, in two different Year 4 groups, girls were willing to play with someone they did not like or who they felt was merely 'hanging around', provided this was what the leader of the group wanted. Eve's body language and tone of voice belied her assurance that, if her best friend and leader of the small group, Sally, chose Mandy as her best friend, it was 'fine by me'. From other comments Eve made, it was clear that she often felt Sally left her with little choice about including Mandy in their friendship:

RG: *If your feeling fed up, who do you tell?*

Eve: *Sally...and Mandy if she's hanging around.*

Another child in a different school told of how she would play with a specific girl only if her best friend, who was also the leader of the group, was present:

Taheera takes Anisha away but when Anisha is away then Taheera wants to be my friend. I feel sad and cross. When Anisha is at school I play with Anisha and Taheera but don't talk to her, and when Anisha is away I don't play with Taheera and she just walks away. (Celine)

So great is the children's need to belong to the group that sometimes they may feel compelled to break their personal moral code if this was in conflict with the code of the group.

RG: *What makes you a really good friend to have?*

Tiffany: *Like, if they're getting into trouble and someone's lying, I tell the truth and...I always play and keep everyone together and don't leave anybody out.*

RG: *When you said about telling the truth, are you really sticking up for somebody and trying to make sure someone doesn't get into trouble or is it just that you think it is important that everybody should always tell the truth?*

Tiffany: *Sticking up for.*

RG:　　　　　*Do you ever stick up for your friends even when you know they have done something wrong?*
Tiffany:　　*[Long pause] I just be quiet.*
(Individual interview, Year 2)

Tiffany's comments are very different in tone to those of Sally who, when asked whether she would ever do something in order to avoid being excluded, replied:

Yes, sometimes...not always, sometimes....but sometimes I'd say do what you want.

Sally's response could indicate that, as group leader, she was very confident that she would not be excluded and was therefore less willing to compromise herself. Girls composing the 'inner circle' do not appear to have the same secure base from which to operate and therefore, as Chloe, Tiffany, Eve and Celine demonstrate, have to compromise in order to remain within the group.

The discussions with the girls in each of the three year groups, established that the children's friendships were emotionally important for all involved. The positive aspects of friendships were frequently described in relation to the children's feelings rather than in terms of, for example, the games that were played. A recurring theme throughout the interviews was that friends provided emotional support. Obviously, the older children were able to articulate this idea more clearly and succinctly than the younger children:

Anisha [Year 4]: *They're kind to me...When I'm sad they cheer me up.*

Lisa [Year 6]: *With them I can talk, they won't walk away. If I'm in trouble they won't just say, 'Oh well', they will try to understand.*

Since experience of successful friendships seems to offer these children a high degree of emotional support, it was not surprising to hear these same children all using the word 'upset' to describe how they felt following arguments with best friends, or within the group of friends. Nevertheless, the importance and social accomplishment of having a best friend (Nilan, 1991) may come at a cost. For the girls in these groups, the effect of their ever shifting relationships has direct implications for their work within the classroom. For the leaders, maintaining their position at the top of the hierarchy contrasts starkly with their friends' need for emotional support and security. How this is played out in the classroom context is illustrated by the way Isobel remains relatively unaffected by the disagreements which take place during playtimes, whilst Shumi, a member of the group, finds it impossible to concentrate in class: *'cos you always think they're looking at me and laughing but if you are in the playground you don't have to look at them,* and Hafsha, another member of that same group, also finds that her learning is affected by disruptions and fall-outs within the group: *'cos you think about it a lot. You think 'oh, no, I'm not going to be friends with them or I won't make up'*. Anisha, the group leader, does, however, admit to being affected by arguments but chooses not to tell her teacher because she can't be bothered to answer the questions that the incident will provoke from the other members of the class. Davies (1982) has argued that:

> *These makings and breakings serve two important functions, first in terms of the maintenance of the orderliness of the children's world, and second in terms of satisfying their need for exploration and discovery of the dynamics of interpersonal relationships* (Davies, 1982, p. 68).

This view, and much of the other literature which highlights the supportive role of girl's friendships, have failed to take account of the emotional investment in the friendship, and of how 'who is in and who is out' contributes significantly to the girls' self esteem and the potentially negative effect this may have on their academic achievement. Valerie Hey's (1997) work, however, has explored the painful and, at times, damaging dynamics of girl's friendship groups. My research would support Valerie Hey's work in that these younger girls, whilst undoubtedly feeling that the friendship group offers something positive, also find the experience of exclusion distressing and debilitating. This duality was lived out even more painfully by the girls who found themselves on the periphery of the friendship group.

GIRLS ON THE MARGINS

The girls who found themselves on the periphery in each of the groups usually had a strong social link with one, or possibly two, members of the inner circle. This link was often due to outside factors, for example, Lisa and Shumi's mothers were good friends and shared the same perceptions regarding the strengths and weaknesses of their daughters' school, whilst Carol and Hilary both attended the same music school on a Saturday morning. Despite these common interests, once inside school the influence of the 'marginal' girls with respect to the organisation and maintenance of the group, was negligible. Rarely did they penetrate the elite inner circle, but seemed pleased to be associated with the popular group. However, in the friendship group of Carol, Hilary, Nila, Lucy, Emma and Elizabeth, Emma was an exception. She and Elizabeth had joined the group at the beginning of Year 6 and by the end of the autumn term Emma had managed to propel herself towards the membership of the elite inner circle, dumping Elizabeth on route and consigning her to marginal status. Once securely in place, Emma managed to recruit Helen to the group and, in so doing, widened her base of support, potentially threatening Carol's leadership position. In all my observations of the girls at primary school, this challenge from a member of the 'outer circle' was rare. Carol, the leader, dealt with the situation swiftly by aligning herself with Nila and Lucy, peripheral members of the group, and by drawing them into her orbit, increasing their loyalty and diminishing their independence, thereby warding off any take over bid.

Picking on people both within and outside the group was another way the leader managed to dominate. The girl who was picked on could be any individual, most often a member of the periphery, but never the leader. The reason why a particular individual was targeted was not always clear. It might be that the girl had seemingly transgressed the moral code or had become an interpersonal threat (Adler and Adler, 1998; Eder, 1991), or just singled out for no apparent reason. Such 'singling out' was functional to the maintenance of the leader's position within the group hierarchy. For the peripheral members of the group, the passive 'going along' with such derisive behaviour from the group leaders reflected more their relief that they were not the targets on this occasion, rather than any feelings of power the situation may have afforded them. The girls were also well aware of their marginal position in the group and, even though they acknowledged the actions of the leaders and were hurtful to their friends, they knew that in standing up for their friends they risked expulsion from the group.

RG: *Why do you think Lucy went along with the story about your lost rubber?*

Nila: *Well, 'cos they said to her 'Oh Lucy, don't tell, don't tell Nila we did this, 'cos she'll be really cross'. And I think the reason why she didn't tell me is that, because she's like scared of Carol and Hilary and she's scared that they'll sort of think, well........*

Group members like Lucy went along with picking on friends, even though they knew it hurt, because they were afraid for their own status or position. These girls on the periphery became skilful as well as self-effacing, or even self denying, having to make more compromises than the girls who were part of the 'inner circle' in order to stay in the group. Ultimately they became accustomed to existing in: 'a social world where the power dynamics could be hurtful and accepted it' (Adler and Adler, 1998, p. 68).

VIEWS FROM THE OUTSIDE: THE TEACHERS

Teachers' perceptions of the structure and dynamics of the groups had an impact on the operation of the group. It would seem that teachers' responses to the operation of the girls' networks was influenced more by their personal beliefs and values about the girls' friendships, rather than a school ethos which may have resulted in, for example, work on such things as conflict resolution within peer groups. The teachers supported the girl leader's view of themselves as victims of their popularity, these girls commented on how they felt compromised trying to keep everyone happy. In a group interview Isobel complained:

The thing is, when you lot have an argument I'm in the middle and I don't know what to do.

Their teachers, wittingly or unwittingly, colluded in this perception. As Paul, the Year 2 teacher, said: *Poor Jane is stuck in the middle. Chloe wants to take Jane away to play on her own, so does Tiffany and poor Jane just doesn't know which way to turn.* Whilst Mary, Anisha's teacher, perceived her as: *a diplomat who will do anything to keep people happy........Anisha sometimes chooses to work with a boy sitting next to her rather than a girl because it is easier, it causes fewer problems.*

Anisha's response within the classroom context is perhaps an example of what Goffman (1971) refers to as 'impression management', a skill requiring the girls to ensure that the dominant school values (e.g. willingness to co-operate, minimising conflict and supporting peers) are seen to be maintained. It is interesting to note that the teacher warned, jokingly but within all the children's earshot, that Taheera 'bites'. In so doing, the teacher made a clear distinction between the social skills of Anisha, the group leader, in terms of handling and managing social systems, and her more impulsive friend. The two girls' different responses to situations led me to wonder whether Taheera tended to be aggressive and possessive because of her uncertainty that comes with not being the leader of the group, or whether she was not the leader of the group because she was not so skilled at impression management. Anisha, on the other hand, was so adept at presenting herself as a victim of her popularity that her teacher failed to acknowledge her complicity in excluding a member of the group, apportioning all the blame elsewhere:

I think Taheera could probably be, she finds ways of pushing somebody out, but it's usually more about 'I've got a secret word to say to Anisha now...Me and Anisha have got something special going on' (Mary, Year 4 teacher)

The teachers further enhanced the girls' powerful positions by selecting them to carry out special tasks:

Yeah. Everybody likes her, they like playing with her and like being in her games and she's often the one chosen as the person who will do special jobs............She can be a bit silly at times but she wants to be good so if she's naughty it's just a childish naughty as opposed to a disturbed naughtiness. (Paul, Year 2 teacher talking about Jane)

Furthermore, Paul continued to view Jane in a very positive light, despite the fact that she acknowledged that some of the quieter children could be frightened of her.

The teachers in the study also failed to take account of the effect of the changes in the composition of the group (i.e. who was 'in' and who was 'out'), in that they appeared to trivialise the emotional impact it had on individual group members. It would appear that these teachers, drawing on the cultural ideal of 'real' friendship (Allan 1989), discounted any ruptures to the girls' relationships, brushing aside their upset, assuming that the next day will see a restoration in the friendship. At the same time, somewhat paradoxically, the very instability of the children's friendship creates anxieties amongst these teachers for the children's happiness and well being. Earlier in this Chapter, it was shown how the children are clear about how their friendship groupings can affect the quality of their learning. Even so, the teachers, despite their concern with their children's well being, tended to view 'problems' with friends as no more that an inconvenient disruption to the school day rather than something which could significantly affect their performance:

If they've had an argument in the playground then we'll sort it out at lunch-time and not in the next session, because we've got work to do in the next session and they need to forget about their argument ...it can take some class time so, yeah, that would affect them.
(Paul, Year 2 teacher)

Mary, a Year 4 teacher, observed that:

I know that with that group, if one is feeling left out, there might be sulking going on which will carry on into the lesson ...for example, Celine, whose first language is English, if there is some of the girls not all of them would do this, but some of them might speak in Bengali and she will feel very left out ... but then again that doesn't last very long...you know if I said something to them they'd very quickly snap out of it and forget.

CONCLUSION

What this Chapter suggests is that general understandings of popularity are ill conceived and that the girl leaders in the groups under study were not necessarily the most popular. The leaders however were very powerful. They were socially skilled, manipulative and managed the group's relationships by generating a model of dependency, where their role as leader became central to the effective functioning of the group. The leaders constructed a moral code which demanded loyalty, discretion and trust and to which all group members had to adhere, in order to remain in the group. The grouping of girls did provide mutually supportive contexts for learning and emotional support and offered sympathetic understanding for group members. However, the operation of the group could be terribly destructive to an individual's self esteem and the collusion of the teachers in this process simply exacerbated the situation. The teachers 'took over' the girl's apparent allocation of popularity, but lacked a more sophisticated understanding of friendship dynamics and their effects on individual girls.

The constant battle for the leader's attention renders the members of the 'inner circle' hurt, anxious and uncertain. In each of the girls' groups studied, the leader was always viewed by the teacher as being at least as able as the rest of the group, if not the most able. The structure of groups was influenced by factors of class and 'race', but from the data gathered in the primary phase of schooling, no clear patterns have emerged, it was therefore not possible to make any meaningful and valid generalizations at this point. As more data was gathered at the secondary stage during this longitudinal study, the 'race' discourses affecting the friendship groups were more discernable and are discussed in detail in the following Chapters. Furthermore, the issue of 'stability' within the group hierarchies is not straightforward. Given the young age of the girls involved in this study, it was felt that it was important to value the *girls'* perceptions of 'stability' which, to them appeared to be enduring, rather than impose an adults' concept of stability which operates over a longer time-scale. This approach was adopted in order to enable the young girls' voices to be heard.

NOTES

[1] Thompson, 2002; Hey, 1997; Eder, 1985
[2] Standard Achievement Tests (SATS) are taken by all children in England and Wales at ages 7,11 and 14.
[3] General Certificate of Secondary Education (GCSE) is a national examination take by all children in England and Wales at age 16.
[4] The extent to which a bully can be a friend is discussed more extensively in Chapter 4. Perceptions of bullying differ dependent on the context and time and place, but the form of indirect bullying which manifests itself in the exclusionary practices engaged in by these leaders it would seem allows for a both friendship and bullying to co-exist simultaneously.

TRANSFERRING SCHOOLS, TRANSFERRING FRIENDSHIPS

It has only been in relatively recent times that the perspective of the child's experience of transfer from one phase of schooling to the next has begun to be explored (Measor and Woods, 1984; Reay and Lucey, 2000; O'Brien, 2003).

Until this time, research into primary school transfer tended to concern itself with the organisational arrangements, for example, assessment procedures and selection, with the importance of friendship within this process of transfer being marginal to concerns of academic attainment and curricula demands. In this chapter, I explore the perspectives of the girls in this study as they transfer from their primary to their secondary schools and argue that children lay far greater emphasis on the importance of having, not only a best friend, but also in the significance that they attach to peer group membership at this point in their schooling. As schools are seen as one of the major sites where peer relationships are formed, as well as the arena where future social identities are shaped (George and Pratt, 2004), I would suggest that children need such friendships in order to make sense of their new situation and in the development of their own identity.

In this Chapter, I will document the extent to which the girls' existing social relationships are disrupted as they adapt to and engage with a new school setting. Interviews, conducted during the final year of primary school and at the end of the first term and third term of secondary school, identify the girls' concerns regarding their experiences of friendship. I examine the priorities of the girls and suggest that schools do not take sufficient account of them and, instead, privilege organisational structures, a prescribed curriculum against a background of school improvement.

STUDIES OF TRANSFER

Measor and Wood's (1984) highly celebrated ethnographic study of transition was one of the first studies to acknowledge the importance of friendship within the process. Their study focused on the pupil's attitudes to transfer rather than the teacher's, and explored the whole experience of transition from the pupil's perspective and found that for the pupils, the last term in the primary school was characterised by high anxiety, tinged with excitement and 'optimistic expectation'. The children in their study used words like 'being frightened', 'worried', ' nervous' and 'scared' to describe their feelings prior to transfer. These concerns in particular were related to bullying by older children, their new status and their separation from friends. Measor and Woods argued that what is at stake over transfer is questions about the children's identity, where the children shift from the 'cosy' world of the primary school to what they perceive as the large hostile world of the secondary school. They maintain that in making adjustments, the children evaluate themselves against others, particularly those within their friendship networks. Thus, making friends during the early weeks in their new school was very important.

More extensive evidence on children's reactions to school transfer comes from a study by Ruddock, et al (1996). Ruddock and her colleagues found that pupils did not find the transition as difficult as some earlier studies have reported (Delamont and Galton, 1986), but rather suggests that the transfer process is part of a bigger issue and a much longer process, whereby children come to terms with their identity and status as secondary school students. She argued that Year 8 in particular, is a significant year, since it often lacks a key identity, coming as it does before the Standardised Assessment Tests (SATs) in Year 9, followed by two years of intensive preparation for 16+ examination, and lacking the 'novelty' of the transfer year. Ruddock's research found that Year 8 is regarded by many pupils as a 'fallow year', in which the dynamics of friendship groups become all-consuming' (Ruddock et al., 1996). This longer process of transfer thus becomes one where children move from one school year to the next, and at each transition point they meet new teachers and have to face fresh challenges in their work. Ruddock suggests that this brings with it the danger that some students will be increasingly unable to manage their learning and, for some, this will mean they will fall further and further behind. This study reflects Ruddock's study in so far as the shift in leadership and other roles within the friendship group became more apparent during Year 8. However, my research also found that friendship was a critical issue for the girls at the point of transfer and beyond, for the girls perceived that friendship would help and support them when moving and adjusting to their new secondary schools.

A recent ORACLE replication study (Galton, et. al., 1999) found that many of the features of transfer identified twenty years earlier by Galton and Willcocks (1983) were still very much in evidence. Secondary teachers still held fast to the view that primary teachers were undemanding and that primary school children have very limited exposure to 'sophisticated' forms of learning. Galton et al (2000) note that these tendencies for teachers to hold onto stereotypical views about what goes on in either the primary or secondary school, 'the other school' has implications for those children at risk. For example, Hargreaves and Galton (2003) found that primary teachers identified those children at risk from among those who were socially isolated, or had few friends, if any. Whilst after transfer, children who underachieved were seen as problem children. This echoes Ruddock's 1996 study where children who were identified as failing, not because they lacked potential, but because they had made unsatisfactory friendships and had not received the necessary support because, in making judgements, teachers were found to be operating at the level of generality. These stereotypical views lend further credence to the notion that children at secondary school have to 'fit in' and adjust to a rigid and regulated arrangement. The organisational structures, I would argue, have no relevance if they are not learner centred, for, as Ruddock's study suggests, the children who don't 'fit in' become pathologised as inadequate. These more recent studies bring into focus the need to foreground the emotional and social concerns of the child and the importance of the role of friendship, both at the point of transfer and in adapting to the secondary school culture.

There have very recently been studies, which have focused on transfer and aspects of gender and identity within the process. Reay and Lucey's (2000) study of identities at transition challenges earlier studies, which prioritised the negative and pessimistic aspects of transfer. Instead, they explored how both the experience of anxiety and excitement that was evident in the children's accounts of transfer, can contribute productively to the anticipation of 'future possibilities'. And working with the children who were going through the process of transfer, they found that:

> *Despite the very great fears which children at times expressed in relation to the move from primary to secondary school and challenges which the new environment will present to them, there was much evidence to suggest that most are able to call on hopeful feelings that on some level, at least some of the time, that move will be a benign one, populated by people who will be willing and able to support them through changes* (Reay and Lucey, 2000, p. 203).

The refreshing optimism of Reay and Lucey's study can be found at moments within this study, for the girls narratives of changing schools are laced with excitement and anticipation of future possibilities. However, for some, their narratives are tempered with concerns regarding isolation and loneliness. Jackson and Warin's (2000) study, which explored the importance of gender in identity formation at key transition points in schooling, found that girls who transferred to mixed secondary schools were less confident than girls transferring to a single sex school. They suggest this is due to their worries about being put down by boys and therefore, at the time of transfer, they form close knit groups for emotional security and safety.

O'Brien's (2003) very recent study on transfer focused on girls' classed and feminine identities. O'Brien argued that although moving from one phase of schooling to the next was a highly significant step for all children, her research found that girls from a working class background felt a greater sense of emotional pain and loss in leaving the familiar surroundings of their primary school and the sense of family and community that the primary school engendered. O'Brien suggests that working class girls' identities are bound within experiences that make the dominant values and academic demands of the school system have less immediate relevance for their lives. She warns that, as the working class girls transfer, despite the excitement they express and opportunity they perceive the move will bring, the transition results in: *a series of exclusions that produces the first steps in 'moving out' rather than 'moving on'* (O'Brien, 2003, p. 265). Within this study, Kate, after one term in her secondary school, was struggling with most aspects of her schooling and may well have 'moved out'. There was also resistance from some of the African-Caribbean girls (this is discussed in Chapters 1, 2 and 7), to dominant views and constructions of femininity, but their acknowledgment that school was the way to gain credentials leading to greater opportunities ensured they 'moved on'.

This review of literature provides the backcloth for understanding and making sense of the girls' narratives regarding the impact that school transfer has on their sense of self, their friends, friendship groups and peer relations in general

THE PRIMARY SCHOOL AND LOOKING AHEAD

Through a detailed analysis of the girls talking about their perceptions and feelings of transferring to secondary school, it became clear, like the children in Measor and Woods (1984) and Reay and Lucey's (2000) study, that the anticipated experience was painful, stressful and created feelings of anxiety, but this anticipated experience was also filled with excitement and expectancy. These conflicting emotions were articulated by several of the girls as Shumi, Isobel and Lisa's comments show:

I don't mind going to secondary school, but I don't want to actually start it. (Shumi)

Part of me wants to go but another part doesn't. (Isobel)

I have these different kind of times when I am nervous about it, I'm really like 'oh, it's going to be too hard, I'm going to have so much homework'. And then it's like 'oh, it's got to be so much fun. We'll have so much stuff to do'. (Lisa)

For all girls, the major differences they predicted as they moved from primary to secondary school were based on structural changes, for example, the size and layout of the buildings, the greater number of teachers and pupils and curriculum diversity.

It won't be the same as it is in Primary school. It will be much bigger. And there will be a lot more things to do and it will be kind of scary – loads of people and different classes to go to. (Hafsha)

And it will be like moving around a lot like because we go to different teachers instead of sticking with one. (Lisa)

Hafsha and Lisa's comments suggest how the intimacy and homely environment of the primary school, and in particular the primary classroom, is in stark contrast with their expectations of secondary school. They already appear to conflate the perceived size of the school and the prospect of meeting different teachers with feelings of fear. However, they were also beginning to acknowledge and accept the impersonal, bureaucratic and regulatory ethos of the school. As Isobel predicted:

Bigger school, all together with children of all ages, stricter rules. loads more homework..

Important as these arrangements were to the girls, by far the greatest issue for them focused around friendship[1]. At the end of the year, when the prospect of going to high school loomed with its highly organisational structures, many of the girls felt concern over what might happen to their friendship group. They felt certain that they would remain in contact with some if not all of their friends. Some of the girls felt that upheavals caused by the new organisation would probably lead to a change in their social relationships. As Adler and Adler (2001) argue, that whilst in the primary school:

'the intensity of the peer relationship is constructed around the restrictive and contained setting of the classroom base, the social system, which on the one hand may allow little opportunity for mobility and escape from unwanted clique attention, does, on the other hand, provide a great deal of security for its' members' (Adler and Adler, 1998, p. 199).

As Lisa pointed out:

......here, in Primary school, you can stay in the same class and all of your friends are in the same class as you. [Yeah] So basically you are always with them unless they are away.

The role of friendship in supporting one's own sense of identity, by reinforcing and reciprocating valued aspects of self alongside the offer of help and security in times of need and trouble, has a particular resonance at this time. The girls had earned respect, esteem and acceptance from their group at primary school and now these aspects may have to be fought for all over again. *'The prospect of marginality in their new school setting, placed the girls in a kind of limbo where understood referents used to identify themselves no longer applied'* (Measor and Woods, 1984, p. 9).

The loss of existing friends and the ability to make new ones was a critical concern for all of the girls. Here Chloe, who was the only one from her school transferring to her particular high school, reflects on her feelings at the end of Year 6:

I was worried I wouldn't make new friends and that I would be the one person in the class who wouldn't be in a particular group. I was worried that everyone in the class would have a good friend already and that I didn't. I was worried I wouldn't find anyone I really liked and I'd have to pretend to be someone I wasn't... to fit in.

Chloe's concern that she might have to pretend to be someone she wasn't in order 'to fit in', like the primary school friendships, highlights the importance of friends in making sense of situations and in establishing one's own identity. The loss of friends on transfer was clearly deeply disturbing for Chloe, for it threatens to dismantle *'the 'props' of [her] support system'* (Measor and Woods, 1984, p. 14)

Some of the girls strategically used this latter part of this final year in primary school to secure closer friendships and form new alliances with girls who had previously been part of another group within their class, but who were now going to go to the same secondary school. Furthermore, those girls who had been tolerated as part of their existing social network, but had been on the periphery of the group, were now legitimately eased out. These responses by the girls re-emphasise friendship as both practical and pragmatic. The culture of the girls' world: *'where pairs group up with other pairs, results in complex social relations. This complexity enables girls to construct new networks of potential friends, whilst breaking off with others'* (Thorne, 1993, p. 94).

As Isobel, the group leader, responded when asked if she intended to stay in touch with her existing group of friends from primary school:

Isobel:	*I don't know, I think I will stay in touch with Lisa. Not so much Shumi because we're really close friends, but were not like, oh, phone each up and give each other telephone numbers.*
RG:	*What about Lauren?*
Nora:	*Lauren, um, well I'm not sure.*

The maintenance of existing friendships groups and the construction of new ones were clearly high on the girls' personal agendas. However the girls expressed differing levels of confidence in their ability to manage either the existing or new friendships. These differing levels of confidence reflected the girls' positioning within the hierarchical construction of their existing friendship group. Isobel, who was positioned as the group leader: *doesn't have to worry [she] gets friends easily.* Whereas Hafsha, a member of the inner circle of the group (see Chapter 4), who was to attend the same secondary school, expressed her anxiety that Isobel may leave her for new friends:

Hafsha: *I don't know. I think she will make other friends but I don't
              think anymore that she'll leave me when we go to Dunwood
              Girls, because she has been my best friend, one of my best
              friends since I was little. So I don't think she would do that.*

RG: *So you think she will stay loyal. Do you anticipate being her
              friend all the way through school?*

Hafsha: *Yeah, umm....... I don't know, umm. I think I will be her friend
              all the way through school but I'll have other friends of mine.
              I don't know. Because we might get other best friends, but if
              we like, have been to the same school all our lives then, umm,
              she is still going be my best friend.*

Such doubt and uncertainty confirms the findings discussed in Chapter 5, that
beneath the seemingly harmonious exterior of girls' friendships, there lies tension
and conflict. During the interviews, Isobel made no attempt to allay Hafsha's fears,
leaving her feeling vulnerable and fearful for her future relationships.

Shumi, a member of the inner circle, expressed a level of confidence in making
new friends which served to mask her insecurity about moving into an
environment, which she perceived as threatening and potentially competitive:

*I think it is hard for people to try and get to know me really, because I kind
of, like, I make it hard for other people to... I don't know. It's just a natural
thing like being aware that you have to get to know me before I actually go
'yeah, I'll be your friend'.*

Shumi also drew upon 'contingency friendship' which, according to Davies (1982),
is a friendship that is called upon when it becomes necessary to leave an existing
friend because of inappropriate behaviour, or in circumstances such as these, where
children transfer schools.

*I will make friends anyway for sure but like starting a new school is
something big and with a friend there it makes it easier. Like, in the way that
it's going to be easier to... I'm gonna feel less scared around teachers and
everything or doing stuff, because my friend will be there. And, like, if I have
any problems and I don't make friends then I can always stick to her and tell
her about different stuff.* (Shumi)

The functional nature of friendship as identified by Davies (1982) is very much in
evidence in Shumi's discussions, for despite the bravado of her initial response, she
recognises the support and reassurance that contingency friends bring.

IMAGE AND STATUS

A concern with image and status among peers appeared to be highlighted at this transitional phase, for the moving from the top of one hierarchy to the bottom of another when transferring schools provided another source of anxiety.

The girls' repositioning as the newest and youngest members of the school community was anticipated as a source of potential embarrassment and worry about being patronised and humiliated by older and bigger pupils:

Everyone says 'look at those sad year 7s'. (Melody)

I won't be the biggest any more. I'll be like the smallest. And they probably will be, like, 'Oh, look at the new people, look at the new people'. (Kate)

Isobel, however, the group leader, expressed it as more of an irritant rather than a humiliation to be tolerated once again:

When I go to secondary school I will be the smallest again. I used to be the smallest when I first joined Kington and now I'm going be the smallest all over again.

A further concern with image and status amongst peers became apparent at this transitional phase, and was articulated by Melody who felt grateful that her sister, a girl in Year 10, provided her with what she perceived as insider knowledge.

It was a real advantages having Katherine in the senior school, she made sure I fitted in and didn't look sad, 'cos everyone says 'sad year 7's'. She told me what bag to get, it had to be a shoulder bag, not a rucksack, which colour socks.......black and the kind of shoes I should wear and that I should wear a baggy jumper, not a tight one and my skirt had to be above the knee .A lot of people didn't know this 'cos they didn't have a sister'.

(Melody was the only girl in the sample who had an older sister in the secondary school she was transferring to)

The girls' anticipated feelings of humiliation because of their size, being the youngest, or their appearance has, according to Measor and Woods, been one of the reasons for the proliferation of myths and stories about prospective secondary schools. The passing down of stories and myths has been seen as one resource for helping them cope with the coming transfer (Measor and Woods, 1984, p. 16). It is these stories and myths, which I now turn to.

STORIES AND MYTHS

The girls in this study had constructed an institutionally defined image of what secondary school would be like; this construction was based on handed-down stories and popular myths from peers, such as terrifying teachers, huge daunting buildings and being bullied by older pupils.

They said if someone tells you that they are going to bully you or kill you, then you must go and tell the teacher. (Heidi)

Heidi's response was unusual in so far as it referred to the physical aspects of bullying, which as Delamont's (1991) survey reported, tended to be found in stories told and reproduced by boys. However, stories about ghosts and the supernatural have been found to be fairly common among girls, and this was the case amongst the girls in this research.

I was told that there was a blue ghost in the school and that it was in the drama hut, and everybody who walked past it, including the teachers, got scared. (Melody)

I heard that there was this ghost of this girl who had been killed in an accident at school, living under the stage and sometimes you could hear her crying. (Lauren)

Delamont suggests that if the new school represents 'the topsy turvey world that is coming, there may well be ghosts [and]...staff may well be ogres' (Delamont, 1991, p. 252). She argues that stories and myths about strict teachers, bullies and ghosts serve to emphasise the status inversion, from being top of one tree to the bottom of the next, maintaining that myths about the sort of hazards new children think they will face from bigger and older pupils serves to humiliate them.

Measor and Wood suggest that 'the content of the myth involves the allocation of status and the legitimation of the power of a particular group or individual' (Measor and Wood, 1984, p. 26), for it is those who have power that usually tell myths. However, Reay and Lucey suggest that the myths and horror stories serve two purposes, one as a defensive strategy, for rather like fairy tales, these myths allow children to explore and examine their fears at a distance. Secondly, as a way of valorising the child's sense of self worth through their choice of school, for the choosing and being selected for a popular school acts as a defence against 'a deeper, more unconscious level of uncertainty that perhaps the school will not be good enough' (Reay and Lucey, 2000, p. 198).

The myths that had been passed down to the girls in this research were greeted with a degree of disbelief, but also with a degree of anxious anticipation.

INDUCTION

A consideration of the type of induction the girls received in preparing them for secondary school transfer revealed quite different levels of support; it also revealed scant attention being paid to the issue of peer relations or the importance of friendship within this process.

The girls' primary school had only informally talked about the process of transfer, for when asked: *in what ways has your primary school prepared you for going to secondary school?* neither Heidi or Lisa could report on any significant interventions:

Umm, told you to look out for things...umm, told you what it's going to be like there and uh.... (Heidi)

Lisa simply responded by saying: *they haven't done anything.*

All the girls reported that they had visited their prospective secondary schools either on the school's open days or at an induction day, and at that time they had engaged in a variety of activities:

Well, it starts from 9.30 to 3.30 and you bring like pencils and rubbers and stuff. And you can try out the lunch and stuff, and meet all the teachers. And then at the end of the day you can buy like school stuff, like rulers and the jumpers and stuff. (Shumi)

They gave us a form to fill out, if I play instruments... stuff like that... if I'm going to be school dinners. (Laura)

They also reported that, in some cases, they had been asked to nominate a friend from their primary school to be in a class with them at their new school:

RG: *Do they ask you if you want to be in anybody's class particularly?*

Heidi: *Yeah.*

Hafsha: *Yeah.... er, no, I... we don't say whose class we want to be in, just like who we want to be with and I said Isobel. And she said me .... well, she told me she did.*

(Hafsa's uncertainty about Isobel's friendship as highlighted by this remark is discussed in Chapter 5)

However, for some of the girls, this question was not one that they could remember being addressed to them.

RG: *Did they ask you to say who your friends are or who you'd like to be in the same class with?*

Kate: *No, I don't .. umm, they didn't.*

The lack of serious concern about the girls' friendships lends support to the argument that the impersonal, bureaucratic imperatives of the school simply exacerbate the pain for vulnerable children already having to deal with a complex set of changes.

In exploring the girls' induction programme what did become evident was the headteachers' focus on issues concerning behaviour, curriculum matters and academic issues, meant that little attention was paid to peer relations or the importance of friendship within the process. As noted above, only a few of the girls were asked directly about friendships, and the only other acknowledgement or concern with 'friendship' was when secondary liaison teachers consulted with their primary colleagues about which girls should or shouldn't be placed together in the same tutor groups at secondary school. The absence of any systematic and direct consultation with the girls in this study, demonstrates the low priority given to this aspect of transfer.

The seeming lack of awareness of the importance of friendship was underlined at an induction evening at one of the secondary schools. Here, parents of prospective girl pupils were informed by the headteacher that the making and breaking of friendships of girls when they entered secondary school was an inevitable part of this stage of schooling, and therefore should not be seen as a cause of anxiety. This headteacher failed to acknowledge the importance that peer relationships has on girls when adjusting to a new environment. Rather, she adhered to an agenda, which continued to place a greater emphasis on the regulatory framework of the curriculum and the behaviour of pupils. Thus, the induction programmes, whilst seemingly useful in terms of providing information, did little or nothing at all to alleviate the girls' real concerns about their friends and other aspects of the informal culture of the school.

NEGOTIATING THE NEW ENVIRONMENT

The importance for all children of having a best friend and belonging to a social group is emphasised in the work of Furman (1989) and Cotterell (1996). Cotterell comments on how the stress of transfer becomes more intense when pupils fail to relinquish their attachments to primary schools. He goes on to suggest that such pupils find it difficult to invest themselves emotionally in a group of new teachers or class-mates. Cotterell further maintains that they need friendship in order to make sense of a new situation and to support the development of their own identity. He sees the school as a major place where peer relationships are formed, as well as the arena where future social identities are shaped.

In the interviews conducted at the end of their first term in secondary school, most of the girls expressed a degree of relief as having survived this initial phase. However, the issues and concerns they expressed in primary school continued to be the basis through which they mediated their secondary school experience. Again, the curriculum did not feature in any discussion, but the social and environmental predominated:

> *I didn't really know anybody and I might not have been in the same class as Laura or Shumi, but it was great, they helped me and I also helped them.* (Heidi)

> *I found that most of my friends from primary school were in my class, it made secondary school much better.* (Melody)

Heidi and Melody's remarks point out that friendships during this first term were still organised around their primary school friends and how the functional aspects of friendship supports them in the negotiation of their new environment. Some girls, like the students in Measor and Woods (1984) study, clung to girls who had either not been particularly close friends at primary school or had been in a parallel class.

> *I sat next to Rebecca on my first day at senior school, we were already kind of friends, not best or anything but we knew each other and we were nervous, but being with each other made us feel secure.* (Leila)

Whereas Kat chose Anna to sit with: *because she went to the same primary school as me but I didn't know her very well.* (Kat)

For Leila and Lisa the primary school connection provided a strong enough link to legitimate a relationship whose function was to provide social and emotional security in this seemingly 'big' and 'scary' and environment.

Whilst others, like Chloe, who had neither friends nor relatives attending her new school, sought out other girls who were in the same situation quickly establishing new but tentative links:

> *Making friends was easier than I thought, because no one knew everyone, it wasn't seen as unusual to just go up and say 'hi, what school are you from?' ....and start a conversation from there. I had spoken to everyone by the end of the first week, I didn't have to pretend to be someone else because everyone was pretty much the same. I soon found my way around the school.* (Chloe)

The speed with which Chloe made new friends provides further evidence of the pressing need for friendship at this critical point in the girls' schooling. A school can feel an unsafe place for those who are alone and the finding of a friend can reduce the chaos of the school (Shaw, 1996, cited in Gordon et al., 2000). This was certainly the case for Chloe.

ONE YEAR ON

As the year wore on, the pupils found that most things were not as bad as they had been led to expect. Most pupils were able to cope with their work. Teachers were, for the most part, as friendly as their old ones, and once they had {mastered} the new rules, the children's anxiety began to disappear.
(Galton and Willcocks, 1983, p. 173)

New friendships formed rapidly during the girls first year at secondary school. As Year 8 commenced, some of the primary school friendships began to fracture and drift apart. New alliances emerged and adjustments and realignments took place (see Table 3, p. 110). In the case of Isobel and Hafsha, the hierarchical nature of their friendship, which had been sustained during Year 7, was now challenged:

I mean, she still likes to think that we're best friends, but I think she knows that we're not really close anymore.....I think the people in our group, I think they find her quite annoying, and she used to be, like, really popular. And she's not popular anymore. (Hafsha)

(The possible reason's for Isobel's loss of popularity is discussed in Chapter 4.)

Whilst most of the girls were very positive about having made new friends, it was only Heidi who reported any personal bullying or harassment:

Well, the first time, I was in the dinner queue and these girls were in front of me. And they just looked behind and started sort of like looking me up and down and then sort of just fixed their eyes on my feet....and then they turned round and they were laughing. (Heidi)

Hierarchies and differences are often solidified at this early stage by marking out those who don't belong or are different (Gordon et al., 2000). Heidi, in terms of her style, the way she wore her school uniform and other bodily signifiers, was different. By the end of the project Heidi's appearance was the same as it had been at the start. She still wore two long plaits and dressed in an androgynous manner. Heidi may well have been picked out by other members of her class as not belonging, but through having a close circle of friends, consisting of Lauren one of her friends from Kington primary and now a leader at Foresters High, her life was made more manageable.

TABLE 3 – Girls' Friendship Groups in Secondary School

Foresters High		Foresters High		Park Avenue		Dunwood Girls	
Year 7/8		**Year 7/8**		**Year 7/8 ***		**Year 7/8**	
Danielle	L	**Lauren**	L	**Leila**		**Hafsha**	L
Shumi	I/C	**Heidi**	I/C	Rebecca		Gretal	I/C
Maxine	I/C	Emily	I/C	Emma		Csilla	I/C
Nadine	P	Beth	P			Tilly	P
						Isobel	P

* No clear hierarchy evident in this group

Askey's Cross		Towny High		Sandown Sec	
Year 7/8		**Year 7/8 ***		**Year 7/8**	
Lisa	L	**Sian**		**Melody**	L
Michelle	I/C	Tan		Susie	I/C
Sandra	I/C	Chloe		Pippa	I/C
Bernie	P	Jeni		Catherine	P
Komal	P			Rebecca	P

* No clear hierarchy evident in this group

Key:
L   =   Leader
I/C =   Inner Circle
P   =   Periphery

Bold represents girls from primary schools

Not Bold represents new friends made at secondary school

One of the girls reported that she had not really made any new friends, nor had she maintained existing friendships from primary school. Kate, who had seemingly been a content, academically able and reasonably popular girl, although on the periphery of her friendship group at primary school, had found herself isolated, unhappy and disempowered by her new secondary school. She had felt unsupported by her teachers, who 'don't like me'. So acute was her loneliness, that she was ready to leave the school by the end of this first term. (Unfortunately, as documented in Chapter 3, I was unable to gain access to Kate, either through her school or through her mother after this first term in Year 7). Kate's experience serves to underline the critical importance of making friends for enhancing self esteem and confidence. Her experience also illustrates that, conversely, if you don't make friends, the potentially damaging effect on identity formation, confidence and achievement is immeasurable.

Research reflects Kate's experience, for it suggests that some pupils fail to maintain progress at the point of transfer because of difficulties in adjusting to the new environment, losing old friends and making new ones, coping with a wider variety of teachers and different expectations of the teaching style. As one secondary school teacher observed:

You always notice when the Year 7 kids come in. It's like a whole new way of life for them. If you can make it easier for them socially to settle in then, in my opinion, they will find it easier academically as well...

The dominant policy discourses relating to high school transfer have reflected current U.K. governmental concerns with raising academic standards and sustaining progress. They draw upon research evidence (Galton et al), which suggests that pupils lose ground at the point of transfer:

Pupils in secondary schools frequently see the years between national key stage tests and public examinations as somehow less important, and do not appreciate that working hard during these periods can have pay-offs. They can become preoccupied with friendships and gain a reputation for messing around; pupils who want to change from being a dosser to a worker find it extremely difficult to shake off their old image. Consequently, they may decide to give up rather than catch up. (Galton et al., 2000)

Galton et al's observations epitomise the abrupt change from educating the whole child, to schooling the individual to shape up to a preconceived set of regulatory and behavioural expectations. But, as this study shows, at the time of transfer from primary to secondary school, there is an intensified desire by all pupils to belong to, and be part of, a network of friends. Hargreaves et al maintains that:

Schools must recognise that the peer group is highly influential for young adolescents and that it can be, at one and the same time, both a major distraction and a powerful ally in the educational process. (Hargreaves et al., 1996, p. 12)

From the girls' responses, it became clear that the need for peer support and help became more acute with transition to secondary school. Choices of suitable allies as friends and being accepted as part of a group are critical for survival, and for a reduction in feelings of vulnerability. As the case of Kate above illustrates, non acceptance and rejection by the group can result in long-term isolation and a heightening of a sense of anxiety. The emphasis on the structural arrangements of transfer, as currently advocated, is of little use to Kate; she is simply left to flounder on the margins. Kate's situation draws attention to the practices of teachers and school administrators and their distance from children's feelings and experiences of friendships, and in particular their anticipation or fear and loneliness in the transition stage. Schools and governments need to be more aware and value the pupils' concerns about social issues concerning transition, which, I would suggest, could ease the pathway. It would appear that, for this group of girls, the continuity and development of the curriculum is not as important as the continuity and development of peer group relations and friendships. The fear of being isolated or marginalized would seemingly over-ride any other concerns. As Delamont observes:

> *They fear the loss of friends made in the lower school and an absence of friendships in the new one. Peer groups or cliques are a major factor in adolescents' school life* (Delamont, 1991, p. 64).

CONCLUSION

This Chapter has highlighted the lack of attention within social research that has been paid to the issues of friendship at the point of transfer from the primary to the secondary school. Through an examination of the literature on transition, it would seem that the majority of these studies have focused on the structural and organisational aspects of transfer, with few studies acknowledging the importance of friendship within the process.

The Chapter has demonstrated that starting secondary school is characterised by anxiety and excitement, with issues of friendship being central to the process. Most of the girls in this study were shown to either consolidate and strengthen existing friendships, or form new alliances with other girls who were transferring to the same secondary school as themselves. All the girls prioritised friendship as the key for facilitating a smooth transfer, as well as easing the process of settling in to their new environment.

The secondary schools, however, continued to emphasise organisational structures and the regulatory aspects of the school. This Chapter has shown that the need for friendship at the point of transfer overrides the structures and practices of the school.

NOTES

[1] I have discussed how the concept of friendship has different meanings for different people and how one behaves with friends will differ from one individual to the next and from one group of friends to the next (see Chapter 4). Friendship, rather than a single, coherent and complete event, is processional and not fixed.

CHOOSING SCHOOLS AND CHOOSING FRIENDS

SHUMI AND LEILA's STORIES

CHOOSING SCHOOLS

In the last decade, the focus on primary / secondary transfer has shifted to a concern regarding school choice within an increasingly market –oriented education system. Researchers[1] suggest that choosing a school and gaining a place at that school is circumscribed by social class as well as 'race' and gender, and that those with economic, cultural and other forms of capital use them to secure the best schools for their children at the point of secondary school transfer. Working within an urban context, this study points up the huge diversity of provision of secondary education, which may not be so apparent in a rural area. For unlike a rural area, where the one secondary school is possibly fed by many primary schools, the girls in this study selected, or were selected by, a whole range of different types of schools. In Chapter 3, I describe the schools, one single sex comprehensive school, an all ability single sex foundation school, two mixed comprehensives, a city technology college and a school from the private sector. These schools were located across three London boroughs; such diversity of provision it could be argued is not supportive of social cohesion.

It is interesting to note that, of all the girls in the study, only two transferred to co-educational schools. Kenway and Bullen (2001) observe that gender is now a marketing feature of schools. They suggest that many girls' schools are marketing themselves as specialists in girls' education, with some pursuing and imitating the aspects of the status of girls' schools in the private sector, or alternatively appealing to a feminist agenda where the aim of the girls' education is to fully equip them to confidently take their place in the world of work Not all girls or their parents, however, chose an all girls school for the above reasons, some, for example, Laura and Sian, wanted to get away from boys who interrupted their games, chased them or were generally irritating.

Laura: *Well, it'll be girls. I am going to a girls' school.*

RG: *Did you choose to go to that secondary school?*

Laura:	Yeah. And it's going to be weird only girls, um, I'm going to Foresters High Girls' School, an all girls school.
RG:	Why did you choose that school?
Laura:	'Cos I'm fed up with stupid boys always messing around and that.

Within this study, whilst choice of school was significant to the girls, the data suggests that it was no more important than having friends.

I think it will be sad because I've been here for a long time. I'll, and I'll be moving away from my friends and stuff. And I've known them from when I was in reception. (Shumi)

Hafsha:	I don't know. Like we did an exam because we, I didn't know if I was going to go there, we just wanted to see if I was going to get in. But I really liked it because I did get in and I really liked it so... I don't know. I liked it more than the other schools. And my best friend was going there. So, or one of my best friends, yeah Isobel.
RG:	And one of your best friends is going there. Was that an important factor or not?
Hafsha:	Oh yeah! I wouldn't want to go to a school with no friends.

In contrast, for some of the parents, having a sibling or relative in the school was seen as more important in the choice of schools for their daughters, as Kate describes:

Well, my mum and dad have always wanted me to go there because it's my nearest. It's like you can walk, you don't have to get a bus or the train or anything like that. And my brother goes there. And all my brother's friends go there and I know loads of people there. (Kate)

In the following extract, Heidi reflects her mother's concerns about being sent to a school not of her choosing.

RG:	Why, did you want to go there [Askey's Cross]?
Heidi:	..... my big brother, he's in Year 8 and he goes to Askey's which is quite close to us, my house, sorry. I really, I did like have a look around and I did have this test and I did really desperately want to get in. But they picked, well I suppose...I

> *just didn't get in, didn't get picked. That was the main one*
> *that I really wanted to go to 'cos my brother was there*
> *already. And I do get on well with my brother and my mum*
> *wanted me to go there. So, but then as I just didn't get in I*
> *looked at loads of schools. That was the main one but, then I*
> *went to Foresters High. But my mum is quite scared 'cos it's a*
> *really big school and she doesn't want me to get lost or*
> *anything.*

What Heidi's experience shows is that the notion of parental choice can be an illusion, for in practice in some cases, it is the school that chooses the family rather than the family choosing the school. This adds to the complexity of the study, because school choice is exacerbated by the diversity of provision found in urban settings. The parents of the girls in this study are negotiating a minefield, for as noted earlier, the work of Ball et al (1996), Reay and Ball (1998), and Reay (1998) show that through accruing economic, cultural and other forms of capital, that school choice becomes available to only some parents, usually at the expense of others.

In this Chapter, I focus on the experiences of, Shumi and Leila, as they transfer from their primary school to their secondary schools. Both girls are from minority ethnic backgrounds and both have invested in school success and whilst the process of school transfer was a significant step for all the girls in the study, for Shumi and Leila it was qualitatively different in terms of the way they viewed and approached friendships in their new schools. In Chapter 1, I discussed how until recently, there have been very few studies of African and African-Caribbean girls' friendships and that most studies about girls' cultures reflect the experiences of girls who are white and class privileged. It is this lack of any significant literature on African and African-Caribbean girls' friendships that has led to my focus on Shumi and Leila in this chapter. Within this Chapter the girls' choice of school and their mother's interventions in the choice process are explored alongside the way the girls' approach new friendships, which in Shumi's case, disrupt her teacher's and classmates' conventional understandings of femininity.

THE CONTEXT

Both Shumi and Leila had been part of the core group of friends at primary school and I had followed them from the beginning of Year 6 (ages 10/11 years old) in their Primary school through to the autumn term of Year 9 (ages 13/14 years old) of their secondary school. During this time the girls shared their secrets with me and over time we developed an ease with each other. After the girls transferred to secondary school at the age of 11, the girls and their mothers, Gloria (Shumi's mother) and Janice, (Leila's mother) produced differing accounts of how their ethnicity had impacted on their choice and friendship patterns at secondary school.

The three schools referred to in this Chapter are Kington Primary School, Park Avenue High School for Girls and Foresters High School for Girls. Both the two secondary schools are single sex and within the state sector education sector. Chapter 3 provides profiles of Leila and Shumi and a detailed description of the three schools which feature in this Chapter.

The Mothers

The emotional support and investment mothers make in their children's' schooling has been well documented by Reay (1998). Both Gloria, Shumi's mother, and Janice, Leila's mother, were uncompromising in the emotional support and guidance they gave the daughters regarding their secondary school choice.

For Gloria, the mother of Shumi, her daughter's identity as a young African-Caribbean girl was as important, if not more important, than the dominant values and academic demands of the school system and this had a direct effect on the choice of secondary schooling for her daughter. From my interviews with Gloria, it was very apparent that Gloria clearly knows the value of education but has problems with schooling. Her disenchantment with her daughter's primary school despite the presence of Keith the school's black head teacher, had led her to ensure that her daughter's secondary school was one where the espoused vision of the school placed inclusivity as the core of its philosophy.

> I think Kington was probably the worst school. I mean I couldn't wait to get her to secondary school.... and Kington has got all the trappings of looking like a really wicked school – I think on the surface it looks really wicked....The thing is, Shumi had- Keith was the deputy and he's now the head....its not very multi racial in its staff make up, so Keith being there was a real plus, but he's actually not , that's not his agenda at all....I think I personally did a lot of talking to the school. Do you know what? I think if it was left up to Kington Shumi would just been kind of left, really....I think they were aware of her because I made them aware.
> (Gloria, Shumi's mother).

Gloria's observations would seem to suggest that although the head of Kington primary is black he did not necessarily value diversity, and 'race' amongst a predominantly white staff, was rendered invisible. Gloria's comments also challenge the assumption that because Keith is black he would therefore have an understanding of 'race' and be equipped to tackle issues to do with racism within the context of the school.

Gloria also felt that Keith pandered to the middle class parents and failed to hear the concerns of the marginalised groups.

And the other thing I found with Keith, his responses to parents – and there were some parents....I mean one of the things Audrey [mother of another girl in the group] and I had sussed out anyway was that Kington is quite a middle-class school....a lot of those middle class parents could have paid....they actually sent their kids there for the social aspect....so we'd watch Keith and we thought he reacted and responded to more ferocious middle-class parents because they were more weighty. (Gloria, Shumi's mother)

Gloria's comments place Keith in the same position as many heads in the UK context of having to respond to the current and dominant discourse of the market economy of schooling and in doing so ignoring the needs of the less powerful, those whose voices have less impact.

Gloria was fully aware that Foresters High had worked hard on its equal opportunities policy and that it was implemented very effectively. She was also aware that one of the keys to the school's success was the very good provision for the personal development of students. The production of a confident, assertive young woman who knows her rights was a major consideration in Gloria's choice of secondary school for her daughter as was the local community, which the school served;

the community is important and I was so focused on not finding a school for Shumi out of our area, because I wanted this community feel to continue. I do think it's important to put roots down. (Gloria, Shumi's mother).

Her choice of school was further circumscribed by the confidence she had in the school in listening to her daughter and thereby maximising Shumi's potential. A further influence on both Gloria and Shumi was the knowledge obtained about the school from their extended family, Shumi had two older cousins attending Foresters High.

Leila's mother Janice had brought her children over from Nigeria when they were very young in order that they would benefit from the British educational system. The acquisition of credentials, which would open doors to a career in medicine for Leila, was the determining factor in her choice of secondary school. Janice is fully aware of the process of marginalisation of many minority ethnic children and students in school and also that a 'selective', suburban school would privilege examination success above other kinds of self-development.

I was so pleased when she got to Park Avenue....because you know she is so bright I didn't want her to waste it (Janice, Leila's mother).

She also recognised that high achievement, both academically and professionally, is not only connected to class position but also to racial values and resources and that membership of the cultural majority in terms of schooling is a significant factor in achieving educational success.

> *I was concerned that if she went to Foresters she would get in with the wrong crowd....the school [Park Avenue] you know , well it's the girls' abilities they focus on....they let them develop to the best of their ability.* (Janice, Leila's mother).

Janice therefore felt her choice of Park Avenue would provide the most beneficial schooling experience for Leila in terms of academic success and that issues to do with the development of a strong racial awareness could be supported from the home and the community to which Leila and her family were securely connected. For Janice school is not the site for contesting identity formation.

Shumi, and Leila were not without agency in this process of choice of secondary school. Shumi had wanted to go to Foresters High as her cousin was already a student there and also other friends from Kington would be transferring with them. Leila was also comfortable with the choice of Park Avenue

RG: *Why did you choose to go there?*

Leila: *I don't know like we did an exam because we {Leila's mother} didn't know if I was going to go there we just wanted to see if I was going to get in. But I really liked it because I did get in and I really liked it so ....I don't know. I liked it more than the other schools*

CHANGING SCHOOLS AND CHANGING FRIENDS

Shumi's Story

Moving from one phase of schooling to the next was a momentous step for all the girls in the study, but some felt a greater sense of emotional pain and loss in leaving the familiar surroundings of their primary school and of the sense of family and community that the primary school engendered (O'Brien, 2003). The girls had, whilst at Kington Primary School, maintained close friendships across ethnic divisions. This friendship group had coalesced around Isobel the leader of the friendship group whilst they were at primary school and all had accepted her direction with silence. However, when the girls moved onto their various secondary schools both Leila and Shumi experienced what they acknowledged as a qualitative difference in their friendships from primary school.

The type of friendship I have has changed. In primary school I was surrounded by people I half liked....Now I have closer friends I can absolutely trust and who I can be myself with. (Shumi)

Whilst Leila thought that friendship in the secondary school;

is much better because you have real friends....its about having fun and sticking with your friends through thick and thin. (Leila)

The shift in the power relations that followed at the point of secondary school transfer, found many of the girls in this study stronger and more assertive, this was particularly so for those who difference was defined by their ethnicity. For Shumi, who had been a member of the inner circle of friends whilst at primary school, her resistance to the oppressive structures of her new school became articulated through a seemingly stronger and more assertive sense of self. Shumi, despite transferring to secondary school with two of her close white friends from primary school, had by the end of Year 7 become a member of a new set of friends who were exclusively from the same cultural heritage. In my interview with Shumi during the autumn term of her secondary school, she had already disassociated herself from her two friends from primary school. She was also far more guarded in her responses during this interview than she had been during Year 6 and uncomfortable about entering into any real dialogue with me.

RG: *Have you enjoyed it here so far?*

Shumi: *Yeah*

RG: *In what ways?*

Shumi: *It's been good*

RG: *What's made it good?*

Shumi: *Different stuff and that.*

Shumi's rather abrupt responses could possibly signify that she may have been lonely during this first term at secondary school and therefore sensitive to responding to questions about friendship generally. For when she made her new friends later on that year, Shumi began to speak more openly to me once again.

RG: *So how are things now?*

Shumi: *They're different. Em, I'm closer to different people now...I'm closer to my friend Nadine and other people in my class as well.*

RG: *What happened to Danielle?*

Shumi: *Well me and Danielle are still friends, it's that we're not as close anymore....because I don't really think like me and Danielle are the same type of level and that. But me and Nadine are. We [Danielle and Shumi] don't really understand each other. We see each other but we don't understand each other. We don't really..... now its more me, Maxine and Nadine and sometimes Tasha.*

Shumi's more expansive responses could also suggest that her new group of friends provide her with the confidence for articulating and living out her identity as a black African-Caribbean girl.

The American Association of University Women's report (1991) on girls found that black girls scored highest on self-esteem measures throughout adolescence. These findings are supported by Niobe Way's research, who found in her interviews with urban adolescents of African American descent, that they had a: unique tendency to speak 'one's mind' in relationships (Way, 1995, p. 178), and saw their relationships strengthened, not dissolved by conflict. Certainly Shumi and her new friendship group show some evidence of this, for they were at ease with telling me 'the truth' about their relationships with each other and with their teachers.

I hate her, she's horrible, so horrible, she's just rude to people for no reason.... I don't think you need to be rude to people for no reason and Miss Norris is. She'll come in the class and start being rude .... she's horrible.
(Shumi)

Shumi, in describing her feelings towards her Head of Year, clearly felt no compunction whatsoever to conceal her sense of outrage to me, or anyone else within earshot of our discussions. Furthermore, Shumi and her friends were proud of their honesty and chose not to acknowledge any other way of behaving.

Maxine: *I just say what I feel, I can't hold back my feelings.*

RG: *Do you ever think 'Oh I wish I hadn't said that'?*

Maxine: *No, not really.....I just say it. Cos if I keep it on my chest then it would like haunt me.*

RG: *And do you worry that you might upset people?*

Maxine: *A bit, but then I say sorry to them.* (Maxine, Shumi's friend)

In the culture of this friendship group which valued truth and honesty and which reflects Niobe Way's findings, the impact that such truth telling had on the group's relationships with other girls in the class was quite devastating. Shumi and her friends found their attempts at speaking honestly were either punished by the teachers or rebuffed by their classmates. As Lauren, who was one of Shumi's friends from Kington Primary School, pointed out:

Well, she's black and she's a bit of a racist.... she hangs out with black people mainly. And she's always telling people what she thinks of them, banging on and stuff like that. She kind of classes herself in a whole different class and she and her friends, who are all black, live in their own little world. They're like an attention seekers. (Lauren, Shumi's former primary school friend)

Such resistance to the way Shumi and her friends enacted their understanding of truth and honesty placed them in a dichotomous relationship where they 'struggled in a social desert between 'nice', where no anger is shared, and 'bitch'; they inhabit female identities of assertiveness and truth telling, identities that the culture, and consequently most girls, pathologise as 'mean', 'bitchy'....'
(Simmons, 2002, p. 178).

During these first two years at secondary school the shifting and constantly changing nature of Shumi's identity contributed to a more heightened awareness of her position as a black girl within the institution of the school. Shumi and her friends claimed that they were no longer able to be 'just individuals' but now subscribed to a collective embracing of their 'black identity'

For Shumi and her friends, identity politics often took precedence over friendship, with their friendship group, like Mac an Ghaill's 'Black Sisters and Mary Fuller's girls (as discussed in Chapter 1), functioning to support each other in achieving academic success within an environment they perceived as hostile. The girls valued assertiveness and direct conflict, and this resistance to conventional understandings of femininity, like Mc Robbie's Mill Street Gang, was misunderstood and misrepresented as an anti-school orientation by both the girls' classmates and their teachers. However, like the girls in Carla O'Connor's (1997) study of African American High School students, this group of girls expressed a high degree of racial consciousness and their friendship operated through a 'collective', affirming for each other their affiliation to their African-Caribbean community and also a commitment to academic success. *Their knowledge of struggle did not curtail their academic success but may have facilitated their sense of human agency and facilitated their academic motivation* (O'Connor, 1997, p. 593).

Jane Ward's (1996) research, cited in Simmons (2002), into the role of truth telling in the psychological development of African-American girls, observed that

African-American mothers showed a determination 'to mould their daughters into whole and self-actualising persons in a society that devalues black women' (Simmons, 2002, p. 185). She found that many mothers socialise their daughters to use independence and self-confidence to resist the oppression they are likely to experience as a result of their ethnicity. Ward's observations suggested that 'parents provide their children with ways of thinking, seeing and doing' that is 'transmitted inter-generationally and intended to empower their offspring' (Ward, 1996 cited in Simmons, 2002, p. 185). Shumi's mother was aware that Shumi was learning to walk a fine line between fitting in with the school system and speaking up, this was evident by the several visits she made to Shumi's secondary school to discuss the issues and problems that had arisen through Shumi's 'truth telling'. For Shumi, who is black and British and growing up in a country where the dominant values and discourses excludes and disenfranchises her, the pursuance of success at the cost of her identity as a black African-Caribbean girl was not a position she or her mother was prepared to engage in.

I would suggest, however, that Shumi's mother's intervention fulfilled three roles, one to act as a check and counterbalance to Shumi's behaviour, secondly to ensure that Shumi's chances in terms of credentialism were not jeopardised and thirdly to empower her daughter against racism. Moreover Gloria's choice of Foresters High, an inner city urban school discussed earlier, has enabled both Shumi and Gloria to engage in a discourse of resistance to the dominant values of the school, whilst at the same time accommodating certain rules and regulations thus ensuring the acquisition of potential credentials for Shumi are not compromised. For Shumi her mother's actions signified resistance, resolve and challenge and resulted in her being given a fair hearing. It also signified to Shumi that social injustices can be actively resisted. Had they chosen a different school, for example Park Avenue, with its orientation to academic success at all costs, Shumi's challenge and resistance to the school values may not have been treated sympathetically. Shumi's developing sense of herself as an individual with rights who should be 'respected' by her teachers, may not have stood up against the highly regulated structures of such a selective school leading to possible exclusion.

We don't like being told what to do, ...the teachers got no right to speak to us like that. (Shumi)

Shumi and her friends' heightened consciousness of racism and the structural barriers to mobility may have affirmed her affiliation to her group of friends, but it could have placed her at risk for her future life chances.

Leila's Story

bell hooks (1996) warns against essentialising the experience of black American girls. She reminds us that 'there is no one story of black girlhood' and to imagine that there is a universal minority female experience would be to repeat exclusive patterns of research that at one time privileged the white middle class experience. The experience of Leila, a very high achieving girl from West Africa, lends support to hooks' view. For Leila, rather than being confrontational in her relationships to teachers and school, evolved a more complex response, which involved keeping a low profile, subscribing to the values of the school and being detached from her resistant peers.

Leila: *The school's very kind of multicultural*

RG: *.... in your group of friends is it culturally mixed?*

Leila: *No, its not really, actually. But I don't know why that is. I think it's just cos, we I think we just became friends because we all care about work a bit more.*

Signithia Fordham's research (1988) into the conflict that high achieving black students' experience between 'making it' in school and identification with black culture resonates for Leila. Fordham's study found that the characteristics required for success within the school system contradicted those of solidarity with black culture and thus , for students who wish to succeed within the education system , a strategy of appearing 'raceless' to their teachers and other adults had to be adopted. This resulted in the high achieving black female students perceiving 'making it' as being consistent with the dominant values and attitudes of the institution of the school. The dominant narrative of how to 'make it' emphasises the importance of hard work, individual effort and education. This strategy of 'racelessness' is evident in Leila's commitment to the 'values and norms' condoned in the school context, as well as her rejection of the features of the black community which run contrary to the values of the school, e.g. speaking non-standard English, commitment to group advancement rather than individualism. Fordham suggests that the female students in her study: ' do not believe - nor does their experience support - the idea that they can be truly bi-cultural (Fordham, 1988, p. 83). Fordham argues that;

despite the growing acceptance of ethnicity and strong ethnic identification in the larger American society, school officials appear to disapprove of a strong ethnic identity amongst Black adolescents, and these contradictory messages produce conflict and ambivalence in the adolescents, both toward developing strong racial and ethnic identities and towards performing well. (Fordham, 1988, p. 55)

Thus the individualism necessary for achievement in school resulted in Fordham's students putting a distance between themselves and their black peers and entering into friendships which would maximise their social and academic mobility.

I don't need to talk much. Sarah likes to talk to Alice....and Alice talks to Cheranne and stuff like that. I don't really talk to them about my problems very much; I'm more, quiet.... I have a friend who is really quiet, she doesn't actually talk to people too much....I see her in the library , sometimes working on her homework and I come and sit with her and say Hi.(Leila)

Leila's self-containment ensures her place in this high achieving friendship group and as at her primary school, Leila remains comfortably on the margins of the group. Nevertheless she continues to be a popular member with all her peers as well as her teacher;

In the elections for form captain Leila has come second three terms running....she is very well respected. (Miss Robson, Leila's form tutor)

The work of Fordham reflects powerfully with the position adopted by Leila in school. Leila's mother provides her with a strong support system for her academic success and has encouraged Leila to internalise the values and beliefs taught in school in order to succeed, and like the female students in Fordham's study, Leila vacillates between modesty among her successful peers and a carefully constructed 'racelessness' in front of her teacher and other school officials.

Leila and her friends are like a little intelligentsia. They're the group that are more middle class, more intelligent, more committed to school.
(Miss Robson Leila's form tutor)

Leila clearly acknowledges that resistance to the school structures might endanger herself and her future and compromise her mother's position within her community.

I'm a very quiet person anyway and I work hard and you know, my mum has given up a lot so that me and Ishmail (her brother) have a good education
(Leila)

The extent however, to which Leila consciously or unconsciously has given up aspects of her identity and indigenous cultural system in order to achieve success is difficult to gauge. For whilst Leila's mother placed great store on Leila achieving academically in order to enhance life chances and facilitate social mobility, she and Leila remained firmly connected to her community and, unlike Shumi, Leila was able to express her cultural identity and have it affirmed in many other cultural contexts.

It could be argued that a greater danger to Leila could be that she may become even more silent as she moves into mainstream white academic culture in an attempt to avoid conflict and disharmony and avoid causing the animosity of others who may resent her success. Instead her experiences both in and out of school lead both Leila and her mother to support an achievement ideology. For Leila, whilst her commitment to the 'values' and 'norms' of the school led her to adopt the kind of 'racelessness', which Fordham describes, this strategy was only evident in school and amongst her school friends. Within her own black community, Leila and her family were actively involved through the church, the family and relatives and local community projects.

CONCLUSION

Shumi and her mother are both engaged in the process of shaping schooling to facilitate Shumi in developing her own sense of identity. Gloria is also encouraging Foresters High School as an institution to engage in the politics of identity as played out in a highly urbanised, multi-cultural and multi-ethnic globalised world. Leila and her mother however are choosing the school for providing them with a currency to negotiate choices that would enhance individual worth. Both mothers and daughters are buying into two different outcomes.

The seeming difference in the way Shumi and Leila deal with their marginal positions within school due to their 'race' may stem from their specific cultural locations and community expectations. Both girls, however, know that they are expected to work hard and to use education as a means of enhancing their life chances. It could be argued that both girls are partially subverting the dominant discursive positions of teacher and successful 'white' student, so central to the school, by challenging and repositioning their ways of knowing and understanding who or what is a successful student (Walkerdine, 1981).

NOTES

[1] Ball et al., 1996; Reay and Ball, 1998; Reay, 1998.

THE CONCLUSION

BRINGING IT ALL TOGETHER

In this book I have mapped out and explored some of the ways a group of girls attending multi-cultural, multi-ethnic and urban schools have, through and against dominant discourses of femininities, negotiated their friendships. I conclude that the friendship groups of young pre-adolescent girls are far from straightforward, but are complex, contradictory and immensely emotional. In this concluding chapter, I shall summarise my findings, reflecting on the main points to emerge from this study and look forward to other aspects of girls' friendships that could be usefully explored in further research.

My starting point for this book was my own experience of primary school friendship, where I and others were routinely excluded from the friendship group. I then observed this same pattern of exclusion and inclusion amongst my daughter's friendship group. Through talking to friends I found that this dynamic was a regular feature of these young girls' relationships. I found that this widespread experience was socially invisible and where it was observed the importance of it to young girls' lives was denied or diminished. I was concerned to uncover how girls understood friendship and if their understandings shifted through changing contexts and circumstances. I was also interested in exploring how and why the girls within the friendship group invested the leader with so much power and the extent to which the girls resisted and subverted dominant discourses of femininity to create their own cultural space.

As the research progressed the scope of my study broadened. I was alerted to the role of the teacher in sustaining group hierarchies. I was also intrigued by the conflation in some of the girls' narratives, that a friend could also be a bully. In trying to explore how and why Isobel, Melody and Carol became the leaders, I began to question the degree to which the leader in the group was necessarily the most popular girl in the group. The construction of a moral code within the group and how it was regulated by the leader, and seemingly accepted without question by the rest of the group, was explored. I also paid increasing attention to the phenomenon of changing relationships amongst these urban girls, following primary to secondary school transfer, where the issue of 'race' became a significant theme, emerging at this point in the girls' schooling.

The research developed into a study of the social dynamics of pre-adolescent girls' friendship groups as they transferred from primary school to secondary schools: a small empirical study of friendship using qualitative methods. In tracing through the literature on friendship, I found that there was a great deal of interest in the field of personal relationships emanating from a psychological perspective. However, any advances made tended to be embedded in the domain of the discipline; the dominant concerns were orientated towards the individual, rather than towards exploring the social aspects of friendship (Allan, 1989). This 'psychologising' which stays with the individual brings with it an accompanying expectation that focuses on changing the girl herself rather than challenging the culture. My work is specifically concerned with the social significance of friendship. Whilst I have explored the emotional aspects of friendship, I have argued that friendship is not only a personal matter, but also one which is inherently social. This research suggests that friendship is not necessarily freely chosen, but is contingent on other aspects of the girls lives – Chapter 4 describes how Shumi and Lisa were friends because it suited their mothers' working arrangements. This Chapter also describes how Isobel may have lost her position as the group leader due to the differing structural arrangements found in the secondary school. Thus, friendship needs to be understood against a background of social and structural opportunities and constraints.

THE MAIN FINDINGS

The main findings to emerge from this study are the product of the theoretical framework, methodology and methods adopted, which together influenced the way the data were gathered and analysed.

I want to highlight three key themes that help make sense of the other themes that arise. They are leadership, popularity and status, issues arising at the point of and subsequent to primary /secondary school transfer and how girls resist and accommodate dominant discourses of femininity. As with many of the emerging ideas from this study, none can be contained within the boundaries of a particular Chapter. All of the themes are 'layered' throughout the text (Kenway and Willis, 1993). Ideas and data have been drip fed into the study, occurring in many different places and in different forms, in more or less detail and in a variety of contexts (Mendick, 2006).

LEADERSHIP AND POPULARITY

In exploring leadership and popularity, I found it very difficult to determine what the social cultural resources were that the girls drew on to establish and maintain their position within their friendship group. I could find no link between popularity and group leadership, however I did find that the leader of each of the groups was always viewed by their teacher as the most academically able. This finding resonates with the research of Quicke and Winter (1995) and Eder and Sandford

(1985) which suggests that ability can be a significant source of popularity. I also found that although amongst the groups of friends there was some movement, differences in popularity, power and control separated the positions of the more central members of the group from those on the periphery. For the girls at Kington Primary, their group was structured by a leader, an inner circle and a larger group of peripheral members. This structure was found in the other two primary groups, which were part of the study. This structure was also evident in the sociomatrices in Ball's (1981) study 'Beachside Comprehensive.' Chapter 5 documents how through the inclusionary and exclusionary practices operating within their friendship group, the girls learnt about the dynamics of power and manipulation and also about conformity to the group's moral code. The leaders constructed a moral code which demanded loyalty, discretion and trust, and to which all group members had to adhere in order to remain in the group. The group's stratification system did not seemingly appear to be based on outside factors such as wealth or 'race' but on internal factors of power popularity and status. This stratification was not fixed but fluid and changing, for once the girls moved from the constrained structural arrangement of the primary school to the more expansive structure of the secondary school, other factors did bear down on the group's dynamics. Chapter 4 demonstrates the process of reflection that some of the girls engaged in before forming new alliances. The data, as discussed in Chapter 5, suggests that the girl leaders were not necessarily the most popular girls, but that their position of leader within the hierarchy was mediated through ability. The study found that the leaders were particularly skilled in expressing themselves verbally, they had a very good understanding of the intra and inter group relationships, they were skilled at convincing others to see things their way and manipulating them into doing what they wanted them to do, including their teachers. Indeed as Chapter 5 highlights, the teachers 'took on' the girl leader's apparent allocation of popularity. The leaders managed the group's relationships by generating a model of dependency and their role as leader became central to the effective functioning of the group. One of the distinctive features revealed by the data was that all members of the group had a role which was critical to its stability and coherence. Chapter 4 highlights the ambiguous position of the role of the 'listener' within the friendship groups. As well as developing a dependent following, an additional role of the leader was at least part of the time making the other group members feel good about themselves. The interviews reveal that for some of the girls, by positioning Isobel and her behaviour as manipulative, domineering and ultimately controlling, they positioned themselves as being good and kind. The discourses of positionality, as examined in Chapter 2, allow for the incorporation of power relations and negotiations as exemplified by the girls.

Within this study, there was a link between power and covert bullying. The girl leaders displayed their power in several ways; firstly through their academic ability, secondly through the confidence they had in an unquestioning following from their peer group and lastly also from the explicit support and admiration from their teachers they enjoyed. The findings from this study suggest that the cultural rules by which these girls relate to each other demand that they engage in non-physical aggression. Within the narratives of the girls, it became apparent that the girl leaders invested as much time and energy in presenting themselves as nice and caring to adults, as they did in maintaining their position in the hierarchy of their friendship group. It was the exclusionary practices and seeming betrayal by friends that allowed what seems a contradictory position, that of friend and that of bully, to become conflated in the girls' talk about friends. Walkerdine (1990) suggests that the internalised version of femininity involves girls being 'good' and 'selfless', an ideal impossible to maintain within any relationship; she goes on to suggest that the only way girls can respond is to project badness from the self onto others. It is this 'badness' that manifests itself in the exclusionary practices operating within the girls' friendship groups, leading to a situation where the girls' relationship to femininity and to one and other will be fraught with difficulty. (Kehily, 2002).

Many of the girls in the study seemed to feel ambiguous about bullying. Each one of them expressed concern about it and condemned it, but then stood by and watched it happen without supporting the victim. The girls underestimated the level of their own participation in bullying incidents. As in Margaret Atwood (1988) 'Cats Eye', bullying took a particular form, it was emotional rather than physical, it was subtle and silent rather than crude and obvious. They choose not to recognise that bullying was taking place 'its only light bullying' states Laura, or they laughed it off. The pressure to conform and not be excluded means that, sometimes, the girls would not tackle bullies rather than risk becoming the next victim. Risk and the fear of isolation has been a constant theme throughout the study with the girls choosing to stay and hold onto a destructive and damaging relationship, rather than risk exclusion and loneliness through challenging the word of the group leader, or by attempting to negotiate membership into another friendship group.

SCHOOL TRANSFER

At the point of transfer from their inner city primary to their secondary schools, the girls' major preoccupation with this process was how their choice of secondary school would impact upon their existing friendships. As stated in Chapter 7, the diversity of provision for secondary education, found in inner city and urban contexts, exacerbated the girls' anxieties about their friendships. Chapter 6 describes how the girls believed that friendship would see them through this 'worrying' but 'exciting' time in their lives. This led some of the girls to form new alliances with girls who were transferring to the same secondary school, who until this point had not been particular friends, highlighting the functional and strategic dimensions of friendship.

After transferring to secondary school the girls were still as concerned as before about having good friends and their friendship groups continued to construct rules which all had to accept in order to become a member of the group or remain within it, but as with their friendship group in Year 6, some of the girls' newly formed friendship groups were still not created on the basis of mutual trust or respect but continued to be dominated by a leader exerting her influence over the group. However, as with their primary school friendships, their relationships were contingent on other factors. Two of the most critical in terms of the impact they had on the structure of the friendship groups were, firstly, the different structural and cultural organisation of the secondary school, which led to new alliances being formed and the emergence of new leaders. Secondly, this shift in the power relations that followed at the point of secondary school transfer found some of the girls stronger and more assertive and no longer prepared to unquestioningly follow where the leaders led.

'RACE'

The girls in the study encompassed the diversity of ethnicities found in large urban communities and how the girls managed and negotiated their friendships across ethnic divisions was a core element within the research.

The practices of inclusion and exclusion were part of the process in which the girls were constructed as alike and therefore as friends, while others were constructed as different and therefore ineligible for friendship. Chapter 7 highlights how Shumi had, by the end of year 7, distanced herself from her primary school friendships and formed new alliances with girls from the same cultural heritage. The production of their version of the feminine through 'truth telling' demonstrated how difficult it is to cross the boundaries of what are the acceptable and dominant ways of being a girl and being a friend. Shumi and her friends constructed themselves in ways that led them to be considered by their head of year, their teacher and their classmates, as 'difficult' and 'racist'. The school's response to Shumi's 'truth telling' 'serves to underscore feminist theory (Davies) which points to the way in which female deviance is 'individualized and responded to on the basis of inappropriate femininity' (Wright et al., 1999, p. 305). It is unsurprising that black girls, with their different history and heritage rooted in past racism, as well as different futures dictated by institutional racism, will make friends with girls who share similar backgrounds. These girls carry the dual yoke of sexism and racism (hooks, 1982). Chapter 7 also documents how Leila, a girl of African descent, did not choose a friendship group of girls from the same cultural background. Her strategy of 'compliance' and appearing 'raceless' to her teachers (Fordham, 1988), in order to secure academic success, could be seen as contributing to the maintenance and reproduction of dominant cultural forms.

Throughout this study the agency of the girls has been central in the production of their own cultural practices in relation to their friendship; they have seemingly accommodated the rules and rituals of femininity, whilst at the same time resisted them. They are active in socially constructing their behaviour so that it accords with the impression they seek in order to achieve popularity and acceptance within their friendship group and amongst their teachers.

The theorisations of Carol Gilligan have been useful for this study in leading towards some understanding of how negotiations amongst the girls were framed by the expectations, rules and rituals of femininity. As discussed in Chapters 1, 2, 4, 5 and 7, girls come to know that passionate intimacy and care are positioned as far more important than independence, status and hierarchy. The study illustrates the dilemma that girls face in trying to understand and respond to constructions of friendship idealized by the culture of the school and wider society, alongside a need for recognition of their power, status and independence. For all the girls in the study, apart from the leaders, being caught between doing what is right for themselves, where they become positioned as self-seeking, or ignoring their own needs for the good of others, becomes part of their everyday relationships with their friends. In this study, the girls' declarations of loyalty to, and trust in, each other were played out as a public performance of friendship, with the girls producing themselves as 'good' and 'selfless'. In relation to this, Gilligan's study is limited because, whilst it documents sets of beliefs, it fails to examine how the girls negotiate these sets of beliefs. As stated Gilligan's work has been roundly criticized for its concentration on the experiences white middle class girls, however subsequent work acknowledged that race and ethnicity are key components of girls' experiences. As this study has shown the African-Caribbean girls appear to be better able to maintain a strong sense of self and high self esteem and seem more willing to advocate for their needs and resist the constraining and regulatory understandings of traditional and conventional femininities.

Following Walkerdine (1990), I suggest that the girls in this study were positioned within two potentially conflicting discourses; one, where they are being publicly affirmed and rewarded for displaying the feminine qualities of sensitivity and care and, a second, within which they have to respond to the demands to succeed in school and beyond by being self sufficient and independent. It is possible that the popular girls in the eyes of their teachers and peers, are popular because they can bring off the displays or performances of these two discourses together in a seemless way.

FUTURE WORK.

In this section of the conclusion, I outline and identify themes that would benefit from further investigation and make suggestions for taking the research forward. These suggestions are just some of a whole variety of factors that impinge upon how girls and their friendship groups are constituted and negotiated. The themes outlined below suggest possibilities for further sociological research within the field of girls' friendships. I would argue, however, that with the current explosion of Girl Studies, there needs to be a coming together and a developing dialogue amongst researchers in order that a fuller and more comprehensive understanding of the experience of the pre- adolescent and the adolescent girls is made explicit.

SEXUALITY

An important theme, which I have not directly addressed in this book, is that of sexuality as a major constituent of identity within the friendship group. Whilst it could be argued that sexuality has greater salience amongst older children in the secondary sector, Epstein (1997) and Connolly (1998) have shown that the primary school is also a key site for the production of hetero/sexualities. Although I have not explored sexuality explicitly, it is, nevertheless, embedded throughout this study. Femininities are produced and defined through a 'heterosexual matrix' (Swain, 2000), which through its expectations, regulation and rituals, defines 'the norm' (Butler, 1990; Butler, 1993). Thus femininity and heterosexuality are intrinsically linked and, therefore, all the possible ways of 'doing girl' are actually ways of doing 'heterosexual girl' (Swain, 2000). By not focusing on sexuality within the study, I am not denying its importance but recognise that it was not a direct part of this research.

ACHIEVEMENT

Within the contemporary debates about achievement in school and the focus on credentialism, the extent to which the disruptions and exclusions within young girls' friendship groups impact upon their school success could be an interesting area to explore. For, whilst Power (1998) et al's research found that girls felt 'it was cool to be working', the loss of self-esteem, which accompanied the exclusion from the friendship group, causes academic work to falter. The interviews with the girls highlight the impact this has on their ability to engage in classroom activities and hence their learning; as Shumi remarked: *its like being in a goldfish bowl, everyone looks at you and you can't get on with your work*. Further research in this area would need to address the extent to which girls may deliberately underachieve academically, rather than risk jealousy from the leader and exclusion from the group.

CLASS

As noted earlier in the study, class featured primarily in the diverse make up of the core group of girls, which included both middle class and working class girls who represented the multi ethnic communities found within the inner city. Social class did not determine the girls' friendship group; they were a high achieving group of girls who were supported by both their teachers and their mothers. When the girls transferred to the secondary phase of schooling, even though two of the sample became 'scholarship girls' at a prestigious private girls' school, the effect of class on their newly formed friendship networks was not evident; indeed Hafsha emerged as the new leader within a very socially diverse group of friends. I therefore feel I am unable to make any assertions based on the effect of class on the dynamics of these particular girls' friendship groups. This is not to say that I do not recognise that class has a profound effect on the way children receive and experience school. The high levels of academic achievement of girls attending private schools is founded upon the continuation of class distinctions and the choice of such schools by upper middle class families (Arnot et al., 1999). Furthermore, many ethnographic studies of school and peer groups have been powerful portrayals of cultural reproduction, agency and resistance at work (Willis, 1977; McRobbie, 1978). McRobbie pointed out in her study that both the girls' oppression and their subsequent resistance were gender specific. The girls in her study were working class girls, which meant that both capitalism and patriarchy had negative and interacting consequences for their lives. Hey (1997), in her study of girls' friendships, examined the complex intersections of class and 'race' and illustrated how girls' friendships were 'coded and entangled within the densities and intensities of social division' (Hey, 1997, p. 125). The extent to which class facilitates or limits the type of friendships that are possible and available to young girls is an area that warrants further research. It would be interesting to investigate different groups of girls of similar ages, in different localities and different settings to ascertain the extent to which the regional, class and ethnic relations shape and influence the culture of their friendship groups and their relationship to school and schooling.

Further research could also lead to an in depth study of the significance of ethnicity on the ways of being a girl. Farzana Shain's (2003) recent work on the schooling and identity of Asian girls reflects the findings from my study. One of the group of girls in Shain's research formed an all–Asian friendship group to avoid attacks and abuse at school, but this group also became involved in activities which ran counter to the dominant values and culture of the school. Another group in her study prioritised educational advancement and sought to avoid trouble at all costs (Shain 2003, p. 81). Shain's work clearly resonates with the way Shumi and Leila responded to school and underlines the importance, not only of comparing the differences between ethnicities, but exploring difference within them as well.

One area that was not part of the study, but that has become an area of interest to me as I have worked with the girls and researched the field, is the close link between peer culture to mass communication and commodified culture. Kenway and Bullen's (2001) study of 'Consuming Children' points to the plethora of websites that provide children with the means to 'distribute their voices'; they highlight the potential for their politicisation through such websites as 'Grr Power' (Girl Power) which offers an alternative vision to one that presents girls as being too occupied with themselves and boys to be interested in being political. The recent street action and websites resulting from war with Iraq confirms their potential for the deconstruction of dominant forms of *doing girl* which, as Brian Swallow's survey (quoted in The Observer 7/9/03) observed, girls were involved in: 'high levels of altruism, shown in voluntary and campaigning activities, such as going on demonstrations'. The impact of these 'girl friendly' websites, which celebrate multiple ways of being female and generate images and interpretations of femininity that are reworked by girls through their talk, conversations and daily actions, could be a fruitful area for investigation.

There are other areas I could have explored, for example, I could have studied a larger group of friends and their parents, and considered the impact of siblings on understandings of friendship. I could have moved beyond an urban context into a rural environment and focused on a group of girls moving from the same primary school to the same secondary school. However, the intention of this research was not to provide a definitive study of girls' friendships, but to take a particular group of girls in an urban context and to examine a slice of their complex lives as they were growing up and to make sense of the signs and signifiers as they move from being young children to becoming adolescents.

REFERENCES

Aapola, S; Gonick, M and Harris, A (2005) *Young femininity girlhood, power and social change.* London : Palgrave.

Acker, S. (1994). *Gendered education: Sociological reflections of women, teaching and feminism.* Buckingham: Open University Press.

Adler, A. and Adler, P. (1998). *Peer Power: Preadolescent culture and identity.* New Brunswick: Rutgers University Press.

Adler, A. and Adler, P. (2001). *Peer power: Preadolescent culture and identity.* New Brunswick: Rutgers University Press.

Adler, P., Kless, S. and Adler, A. (1992). Socialization to gender roles: Popularity among elementary school boys and girls, *Sociology of Education, 65* 169-187.

Alcoff, L. (1988). Cultural feminism versus post-structuralism: The identity crisis in feminist theory. *Signs, 13* (3), 405-436.

Alcoff, L. (1997) Cultural feminism versus post-structuralism: The identity crisis in feminist theory, in L. Nicholson (Ed.), *The second wave: A reader in feminist theory*, New York: Routledge.

Allan, G. (1989). *Friendship.* Hemel Hempstead: Harvester Wheatsheaf.

Ambert, A. M. (1986). Sociology of sociology: The place of children in North American sociology. *Sociological studies of child development, 1* 3-31.

American Association of University Women (1991). *Short changing girls, short changing America: A call to action.* Washington: American Association of University Women.

Anyon, J. (1983). Intersections of gender and class; Accommodation and resistance by working class and affluent females to contradictory and sex-role ideologies, in Walker, S. and Barton, L. (Eds.), *Gender, class and education.*

Arnot, M. (2002). *Reproducing gender.* London: Routledge Falmer.

Arnot, M., David, M. and Weiner, G. (1999). *Closing the gender gap.* Cambridge: Polity.

Atwood, M. (1988). *Cats eye.* New York: Doubleday.

Ball, S. (1981). *Beachside comprehensive.* Cambridge: Cambridge University Press.

Ball, S. (1990). *Politics and policy making in education: Explorations in policy sociology.* London: Routledge.

Ball, S. (1994). *Education reform: A critical and post-structural approach.* Buckingham: Open University Press.

Ball, S. (1995). Intellectuals or technicians: The urgent role of theory in educational studies. British *Journal of Educational Studies, 43* (3), 255-271.

Ball, S. and Gerwirtz, S. (1997). Girls in the education market: Choice, competition and complexity. *Gender and Education, 9* (2), 207-223.

Ball, S. J., Bowe, R. and Gewirtz, S. (1996). School choice, social class and distinction: The realisation of social advantage in education. *Journal of Education Policy, 11* (1), 89-112.

Banks, C. and Davies, B. (1992). *The gender trap: A feminist poststructuralist analysis of primary school children's talk about gender.* Junior Curriculum Studies, 24 1-25.

Benjamin, S. (2002). *The micro politics of inclusive education. An ethnography.* Buckingham and Philadelphia: Open University Press.

Bernstein, B (1996) *Pedagogy, symbolic control and identity: Theory, research, critique.* London: Taylor and Francis.

Bigelow, B. and La Gapia, J. (1980). The development of friendship values and choice, in Foot, H., Chapman, A. and Smith, J. (Eds.), *Friendship and social relations in children.* New York: Wiley.

Biklen, S. K. and Polard, D. (Eds.) (1993). *Gender and education.* Chicago: Chicago University Press.

Bjoerkqvist, K. and Niemela, P. (Eds.) (1992). *Of mice and women: Aspects of female aggression.* San Diego: Academic Press.

Blatchford, P. and Sharpe, S. (1994). *Breaktime and the school.* London: Routledge.

REFERENCES

Bourdieu, P. (1987). *Distinction: A social critique of the judgement of taste*. London: Routledge.

Britzman, D. (1993). The ordeal of knowledge: Rethinking the possibilities of multicultural education, *The Review of Education, 15* 123-135.

Brown, L. M. and Gilligan, C. (1992). *Meeting at the crossroads*. Cambridge, Massachusetts: Harvard University Press.

Burke, P. J. (2001). *A feminist poststructuralist ethnography of widening participation*. unpublished PhD dissertation, Institute of Education, University of London, London.

Butler, J. (1990). *Gender trouble*. New York: Routledge.

Butler, J. (1993). *Bodies that matter*. New York and London: Routledge.

Channel Four (March 2003). *Girls alone*. Dual Purpose Productions.

Cherland, M. R. (1994). *Private practices: Girls reading fiction and constructing identity*. London: Taylor Francis.

Chodorow, N. (1978). *The reproduction of mothering: Psychoanalysis and the sociology of gender*. Berkeley: University of California Press.

Coates, J. (1988). Gossip revisited: Language in all-female groups, in Coates, J. and Cameron, D. (Eds.), *Women in their speech communities: New perspectives on language and sex*. London: Longman.

Coates, J. (1993). *Women, men and language: A sociolinguistic account of gender differences in language*. London: Longman.

Connolly, P. (1998). *Racism, gender identities and young children*. London: Routledge.

Corrigan, P. (1979). *Schooling the smash street kids*. London: MacMillan.

Corsaro, W. A. (1985). *Friendship and peer culture in the early years*. New Jersey: Ablex.

Cotterell, J. (1996). *Social networks and social influences in adolescence*. London: Routledge.

Cowie, E. (1978). Woman as sign, *m/f, 1* 49-63.

Darwin, C. (1896). *The descent of man and selection in relation to sex*. New York: Appleton.

Davies, B. (1982). *Life in the classroom*. London: Routledge & Kegan Paul.

Davies, B. (1989). *Frogs and snails and feminist tales*. Sydney: Allen Unwin.

Davies, B. (1990). Agency as a form of discursive practice. A classroom scene observed, *British Journal of Sociology of Education, 11* (3), 341-361.

Davies, B. (1994). *Post structuralist theory and classroom practice*. Geelong, Victoria: Deakin University.

Davies, L. (1979). Deadlier than the male? Girls conformity and deviance in schools, in Meighan, L. B. R. (Eds.), *Schools , pupils and deviance*. Natfield Books.

Deegan, J. G. (1996). *Children's friendships in culturally diverse classrooms*. London: Falmer.

Deem, R. (1994). Researching the locally powerful: A study of school governance, in Walford, G. (Eds.), *Researching the powerful in education*. London: University College London Press.

Delamont, S. (1991). The hit list and other horror stories: Sex roles and school transfer, *Sociological Review, 39* 238-259.

Delamont, S. (1992). *Fieldwork in educational settings: Methods, pitfalls and perspectives*. London: Falmer Press.

Delamont, S. and Galton, M. (1986). *Inside the secondary classroom*. London: Routledge and Keegan Paul.

Denzin, N. (1977). *Childhood socialisation*. San Francisco: Jossey-Bass.

Eder, D. (1985). The cycle of popularity: Interpersonal relations among female adolescents, *Sociology of Education, 58* 154-165.

Eder, D. (1991). The Role of teasing in adolescent peer group culture, *Sociological Studies of Child Development, 4* 181-197.

Eder, D. and Sandford, S. (1986). The development and maintenance of interactional norms amongst early adolescents, *Sociological Studies of Child Development, 1* 283-300.

Edwards, R. (1993). *Mature women students: Separating or connecting family and education*. London: Taylor Francis.

Ellsworth, E. (1997). *Teaching positions: Difference, pedagogy and the power of address*. New York: Teachers College Press.

Epstein, D. (1993). *Changing classroom cultures: Anti-racism, politics and schools*. Stoke-on-Trent: Trentham Books.

Epstein, D. (1997). Boyz own stories: Masculinities and sexualities in school, *Gender and Education, 9* 105-115.

Evans, J. (1995). *Feminist theory today, an introduction to second wave feminism*. London: Sage.

Fine, G. (1981). Friends impression management and preadolescent behaviour, in Asher, S. and Gottman, J. (Eds.), *The development of children's friendships*. New York: Cambridge University Press.

Fordham, S. (1988). Black students success: Pragmatic strategy or pyrrhic victory?, *Harvard Educational Review, 58* 54-84.

Fordham, Signithia (1995) *Blacked out: Dilemmas of race, identity, and success at Capital High*. Chicago: University of Chicago Press.

Foucault, M. (1977). *Discipline and punishment*. Harmondsworth: Penguin.

Foucault, M. (1978). *The history of sexuality*. Harmondsworth: Penguin.

Foucault, M. (1982). *The subject and power*. Hertfordshire: Harvester.

Foucault, M. (1984). Truth and power, in Rabinow, P. (Ed.), *The Foucault reader*. London: Penguin.

Foucault, M. (1991). *Discipline and punishment: The birth of the prison*. London: Penguin Books.

Francis, B. (1996). *Children's constructions of gender, power and adult occupation*. unpublished PhD dissertation, University of North London.

Francis, B. (1998). *Power plays: Primary school children's construction of gender, power and adult work*. Stoke on Trent: Trentham Books.

Frazer, L. (1988). Teenage girls talking about class, *Sociology, 22* (3), 343-358.

Frones, I. (1995). *Among peers*. Oslo: Scandinavian Press.

Fuller, M. (1980). Black girls in a London comprehensive school, in Deem, R. (Ed.), *Schooling for women's work*. London: Routledge and Kegan Paul.

Furman, W. (1989). The development of children's social networks, in Belle, D. (Ed.), *Children's networks and social supports*. New York: Wiley.

Galton, M. (1999). *The impact of school transitions and transfer on pupil progress and attainment*. London: DfEE.

Galton, M., Morrison, I. and Pell, T. (2000). Transfer and transition in England schools: Reviewing the evidence, *International Journal of Educational Research, 33* (4), 341-363.

Galton, M. and Willcocks, J. (Eds.) (1983). M*oving from the primary classroom*. London: Routledge and Keegan Paul.

Garfinkel, H. (1967). *Studies in ethnomethodology*. New York: Prentice Hall.

George, R. and Pratt, S. (2005). Transferring friendship: Girls' and boys' friendships in the transition from primary to secondary school. *Children and Society, 19* (1), 16-26.

Gillborn, D. (1990). *'Race', ethnicity and education: Teaching and learning in multi-ethnic schools*. London: Unwin Hyman/Routledge.

Gilligan, C. (1982). *In a different voice; Psychological theory and women's development*. Cambridge, Massachusetts: Harvard University Press.

Gilligan, C. (1995). The centrality of relationship in psychological development: A puzzle, some evidence, and a theory in Blair, M., Holland. J. and Sheldon, S. (Eds.), *Identity and diversity. gender and the experience of education*. Clevedon: Multilingual Matters in association with The Open University.

Gilligan, C., Lyons, N. P. and Hamner, T. J. (1990). *Making connections: The relational world of adolescent girls at Emma Willard school*. Massachusetts: Harvard University Press.

Glaser, B. J. and Strauss, A. L. (1967). *The discovery of grounded theory*. New York: Aldine Publishing Company.

Goffman, E. (1971). *The presentation of the self in everyday life*. Garden City: Doubleday.

Goffman, I. (1976). Gender display, *Studies in the Anthropology of Visual Communication, 3* 69-77.

141

REFERENCES

Gordon, T., Holland, J. and Lahelma, E. (2000). *Making spaces: Citizenship and difference in schools*. Basingstoke: MacMillan Press Ltd.

Hall S. and Jefferson, T., (Eds.) (1980) Resistance through rituals: Youth subcultures in post-war Britain, London: Routledge.

Haralambos, H. a. (1995). *Sociology themes and perspectives*. London: Collins Educational Press.

Hargreaves, A., Earl, L. and Ryan, J. (1996). *Schooling for change: Reinventing education for early adolescence*. London: Falmer.

Hargreaves, A. and Galton, M. (Eds.) (2003). *Moving from the primary classroom: 20 years on*. London: Routledge and Keegan Paul.

Hartup, W. (1983). Peer relations, in Heatherington, E. M. (Ed.), *Handbook of child psychology: socialization, personality and social development*. New York: Wiley.

Hartup, W. (1996). The Company they keep: Friendships and their developmental significance, *Child Development, 67* 1-13.

Henry, J. (1963). *Culture against man*. Random House.

Hey, V. (1997). *The company she keeps*. Buckingham: Open University Press.

Hodge, G. (1993). Bullying - An issue of inequality, in George, R. (Ed.), *Equal opportunities in schools: Principles, policy and practice*. Harlow: Longman.

Hollway, W. (1984). Gender difference and the production of subjectivity, in Henriques, J. H., Urwin, W., Venn, C. and Walkerdine, V. (Eds.), *Changing the subject: Psychology, social regulation and subjectivity*. London: Methuen.

hooks, b. (1982). *Aint I a woman, black women and feminism*. London: Pluto Press.

hooks, b. (1990). *Yearning: Race, gender and cultural politics*. Boston: South End Press.

hooks, b. (1996). *Borne black: Memories of girlhood*. New York: Henry Holt & Co.

Hughes, L. (1988). 'But that's not really mean': Competing in a cooperative mode, *Sex Roles, 19* 669-687.

Jackson, C. and Warin, J. (2000). The importance of gender as an aspect of identity at key transition points in compulsory education, *British Educational Research Journal, 26* (3), 383-391.

James, A. (1993). *Childhood identities*. Edinburgh: Edinburgh University Press.

Jones, A. (1993). 'Becoming a 'girl': Poststructuralist suggestions for educational research, *Gender and Education, 5* (2), 261-269.

Jones, A. (1997). Teaching post-structuralist feminist theory in education: Student resistances, *Gender and Education, 9* 261-269.

Kehily, M. (2002). Private girls and public worlds: producing femininities in the primary school, *Discourse, 23* (2).

Kehily, M., J., Mac An Ghaill, M., Epstein, D. and Redman, P.(2002) Private girls and public worlds: producing femininities in the primary school, *Discourse: Studies in the Cultural Politics of Education, 23*:2, 167 -177

Kenway, J. and Bullen, E. (2001). *Consuming children*. Buckingham: Open University Press.

Kenway, J. and Willis, S. (1993). *Telling tales: Girls and schools changing their ways*. Canberra: Australian Government Publishing Service.

Kenway, J., Willis, S., Blackmore, J. and Rennie, L. (1994). Making 'hope practical' rather than 'despair convincing': Feminist post-structuralism, gender reform and educational change, *British Journal of Sociology of Education, 15* (2), 187-210.

Kohlberg, L. (1978). *The philosophy of moral development: moral stages and the idea of justice*. San Fransisco: Harper Row.

Kutnick, P. and Kington, A. (2005). Grouping of pupils in secondary school classrooms: Possible links between pedagogy and learning. *Social Psychology of Education, 8* (4) 349-374.

La Fontaine, J. (1991). *Bullying: The child's view*. Gulbenkian Foundation.

Lees, S. (1986). *Losing out: Sexuality and adolescent girls*. London: Hutchinson.

Leonard, D. (1980). *Sex and generation*. London: Tavistock.

Lever, J. (1978). Sex differences in the complexity of children's play and games. *American Sociological review, 43* 471-483.

142

Llewellyn, M. (1980). Studying girls at school: The implications of confusion, in Deem, R. (Ed.), *Schooling for women's work*. London: Routledge.

Lukes, S. (Ed.) (1986). *Power*. Oxford: Blackwell.

Mac an Ghaill, M. (1988). *Young, gifted and black*. Milton Keynes: Open University Press.

Maclure, M. (2003). *Discourse in social and educational research*. Buckingham: Open University Press.

Magezis, J. (1996). *Teach yourself women's studies*. London: Hodder Headline.

Maguire, M., Waldridge, T and Pratt-Adams, S. (2006). *The urban primary school*. Berkshire: Open University Press.

Maher, F. A. and Tetreault, M. (1994). *The feminist classroom*. New York: Basic Books.

Mahony, P. and Hextall, I. (1997). *Teaching in the managerial state*. University of Queensland.

Maltz, D. N. and Borker, R. A. (1982). A socio-cultural approach to male-female misconnection, in Gumprez, J. (Eds.), *Language and social identity*. Cambridge: Cambridge University Press.

Mauthner, M. (1998). *Kindred spirits: Stories of sister relationships*. unpublished PhD dissertation, Institute of Education, University of London.

Mauthner, M. (2002). *Sistering: Power and change in female relationships*. Basingstoke: Palgrave MacMillan.

Maynard, M. (1995). Beyond the 'big three': The development of feminist theory into 1990's, *Women's History Review, 4* (3), 259-281.

McLeod, J. (2002). Working out intimacy - Young people and friendship in an age of reflexivity, *Discourse, 23* (2).

McRobbie, A. (1978). Working class girls and the culture of femininity, in Group, W. s. S. (Ed.), *Women take issue: Aspects of women's subordination*. London: Hutchinson.

McRobbie, A. (1980). Settling accounts with subculture. *Screen Education. 34.* 37-49.

McRobbie, A. (1981). Just like a Jackie story, in McRobbie, A. and McCabe, T. (Eds.), *Feminism for girls: An adventure story*. London: Routledge & Keegan Paul.

McRobbie, A. (1991). *Feminism and youth culture*. Basingstoke: Hampshire.

Measor, L. and Woods, P. (1984). *Changing schools: Pupil perspectives on transfer to a comprehensive*. London: Open University Press.

Mehan, H. and Woods, H. (1975). *The reality of ethnomethodology*. New York: Wiley.

Mendick, H. (2006). *Masculinities in mathematics*. Berkshire: Open University Press..

Meyenn, R. J. (1980). School girl's peer groups, in Woods, P. (Ed.), *Pupil strategies*. London, Croom Helm.

Miller, J. (1990) *Seductions: Studies in reading and culture*. London: Virago.

Miller, J. (1995). Trick or treat? The autobiography of the question, *English Quarterly, 27* 22-26.

Millet, K. (1970). *Sexual politics*. New York: Avon Books.

Mirza, H. (1992). *Young female and black*. Buckingham: Open University Press.

Mitchell, J. (1971). *Woman's estate*. Harmondsworth: Penguin.

Moore, A., George, R. and Halpin, D. (2002). The developing role of the head teacher in English schools, *Educational Management and Administration, 30* (2), 175-188.

Morrison, T. (1974). *Sula*. Allen Lane.

Nilan, P. (1991). Exclusion, inclusion and moral ordering in two girl's friendship groups, *Gender and Education, 3* (1).

Oakley, A. (1972). *Gender and society*. London: Maurice Temple Smith.

O'Brien, M. (2003). Girls and transition to second-level schooling in Ireland: 'Moving on' and 'moving out', *Gender and Education, 15* (3), 249-266.

O'Connor, C. (1997). Dispositions toward (collective) struggle and educational resilience in the inner city; a case analysis of six African-American High School Students, *American Educational research journal, 34* (4), 593-629.

Oliker, S. J. (1989). *Best friends and marriage: Exchange among women*. Berkeley and Los Angeles: University of California.

REFERENCES

Ortner, S. B. and Whitehead, H. (Eds.) (1981). *Sexual meanings: The cultural construction of gender and sexuality*. Cambridge: Cambridge University Press.

Paechter, C. (1998). *Educating the other*. London: Falmer Press.

Piaget, J. (1965). *The moral judgement of the child*. New York: Free Press.

Power, S., Whitty, G., Edwards, T. and Wigfall, V. (1998). Schoolboys and schoolwork: Gender identification and academic achievement, *International Journal of Inclusive Education, 2* (2), 135-153.

Pringle, R. and Watson, S. (1992). Women's interests and the post structural state, in Barratt, M. and Phillips, A. (Eds.), *Destabilising theory, contemporary feminist debates*. Cambridge: Polity Press.

Proweller, A (1998) *Constructing female identities: Meaning making in an upper middle class youth culture*. Albany, New York: State University of New York Press.

Quicke, P. and Winter, C. (1995). Best friends: A case study of girl's reactions to an intervention designed to foster collaborative work. *Gender and Education, 7* (3).

Reay, D. (1998). *Class work: Mothers' involvement in their children's schooling*. London: UCL Press.

Reay, D. (2001) 'Spice girls', 'nice girls', 'girlies' and 'tomboys': Gender discourses, girls cultures and femininities in the primary classroom, *Gender and Education, 13*(2), 153–166.

Reay, D. and Ball, S. J. (1998). 'Spoilt for shoice': The working classes and education markets, Oxford *Review of Education, 23* (1), 89-101.

Reay, D. and Lucey, H. (2000). Children, school choice and social differences, *Educational Studies, 26* (1), 83-100.

Reinharz, S. (1992). *Feminist methods in social research*. Oxford: Oxford University Press.

Reis, H. T. and Shaver, P. (1988). Intimacy as an interpersonal process, in Duck, S. (Ed.), *A handbook of personal relationships*. Chichester: Wiley.

Roland, R. (1989). *Bullying: An international perspective*. London: Fulton.

Rubin, Z. (1985). *Just friends*. New York: Harper Row.

Ruddock, J., Chaplain, R. and Wallace, G. (Eds.) (1996). *School improvement; What can pupils tell us?* London: David Fulton.

Sayer, A. (2005) Class, moral worth and recognition. *Sociology 39* (5) 947-963.

Schofield, J. (1981). Complementary and conflicting identities: Images and interaction in an interracial school, in Asher, S. and Gottman, J. M. (Eds.), *The development of children's friendship*. New York: Cambridge University Press.

Shain, F. (2003). *The schooling and identity of Asian girls*. Staffordshire: Trentham Books.

Shaw, J. (1996). *Education, gender and anxiety*. London: Taylor and Francis.

Simmons, R. (2002). *Odd girl out*. New York: Harcourt Inc.

Skeggs, B. (1992) The cultural production of 'learning to labour', in: A. Beezer & M. Barker (Eds.) Reading into Cultural Studies. London: Routledge.

Skeggs, B. (1997) Formations of class and gender; Becoming respectable. London :Sage.

Skelton, C. (2001). *Boys: Masculinities and primary education*. Buckingham: Open University Press.

Stanley, L. and Wise, S. (1993). *Breaking out again: Feminist ontology and epistemology*. London: Routledge.

Steinberg, L. (1986). Latchkey children and susceptibility to peer pressure: An ecological analysis, *Developmental Psychology, 22* 433-439.

Swain, J. (2000). *An ethnographic study into the constructions of masculinity of 10-11 year old boys in three junior schools*. unpublished PhD dissertation, Institute of Education London University.

Swallow, B. (2003). Lads, friends, love and Newcastle United, in Hill, A. (Ed.), So do you know what your 13-year-olds doing now? London: *The Observer*, 7.9.03.

Talai, A. (1995). The waltz of sociability: Intimacy, dislocation and friendship in a Quebec high school, in Talai, A. and H. Wuff (Eds.), *Youth cultures a cross cultural perspective*. London: Routledge.

Tannen, D. (1991). *You just don't understand: Women and men in conversation*. London: Virago.

Tattum and Herbert (1990). *Bullying: A positive response*. Cardiff: SGIHE.

Thompson (2002). *Best friends worst enemies*. Bury St Edmonds: Penguin.

Thorne, B. (1993). *Gender play: Girls and boys in school*. Buckingham: Open University Press.

144

Tiger, L. (1969). *Men in groups*. Thomas Nelson and Sons.

Troyna, B. and Hatcher, R. (1992). *Racism in children's lives: A study of mainly white primary schools*. London: Routledge.

Waksler, F. C. (Ed.) (1991). S*tudying the social worlds of children: Sociological readings*. London: Falmer Press.

Walby, S. (1992). *Post-post-modernism? Theorizing social complexity*. Cambridge: Polity Press.

Walkerdine, C. S. V. (1985). *Language gender and childhhood*. London: Routledge.

Walkerdine, V. (1981). Sex, power and pedagogy, *Screen Education, 38* 14-24.

Walkerdine, V. (1988). *The mastery of reason*. London: Routledge.

Walkerdine, V. (1989). *Counting girls out*. London: Virago.

Walkerdine, V. (1990). *Schoolgirl fictions*. London: Verso.

Walkerdine, V. (1994). Femininity as performance, in Stone, L. (Ed.), *The education feminist reader*. London: Routledge.

Ward, J. V. (1996). Raising resistors: The role of truth telling in the psychological development of African American girls, in Ross Leadbeater, B. and Way, N. (Eds.), U*rban girls: Resisting stereotypes, creating identities*. New York: New York University Press.

Way, N. (1995). Can't you see the courage, the strength that I have? Listening to urban adolescent girls speak about their relationships, *Psychology of Women Quarterly, 19* (1), 107-28.

Weedon, C. (1987). *Feminist practice and poststructuralist theory*. Oxford: Basil Blackwell.

Weiner, G. (1994). *Feminisms in education: An introduction*. Milton Keynes: Open University Press.

West, C. and Zimmerman, D.H. (1987). Doing gender, *Gender and Society, 1* (2), 125-151.

White, P. (1990). Friendship and education, *Journal of Philosophy of Education, 24* (1), 81-91.

Willis, P. (1977). *Learning to labour: How working class children get working class jobs*. Farnborough: Saxon House.

Wright, C., Weekes, D. and McGlaughlin, A. (1999). Gender-blind racism in the experience of schooling and identity formation, *International Journal of Inclusive Education, 3* (4), 293-307.

SUBJECT INDEX

R

S

AUTHOR INDEX

TRANSGRESSIONS: CULTURAL STUDIES AND EDUCATION

TEACHING, LEARNING AND OTHER MIRACLES

Grace Feuerverger
OISE, University of Toronto, Canada

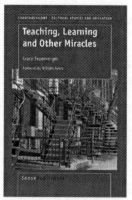

Award-winning author Grace Feuerverger explores teaching and learning in schools as a sacred life journey, a quest toward liberation. Written for teacher/educators who wish to make a real difference in the lives of their students, this book speaks to everyone who finds themselves, as she did, on winding and often treacherous paths, longing to discover the meaning and potential in their professional lives at school. A child of Holocaust survivors, Feuerverger wrote this book to tell how schools can be transformed into magical places where miracles happen. In an era of narrow agendas of 'efficiency' and 'control,' this book dares to suggest that education is and should always be about uplifting the human spirit.

"It is in the spirit of resistance and hope that Feuerverger goes in search of a more fully humanistic pedagogy... A book of inspiration and practical guidance...Here, indeed, is a book about miracles -- written by a miracle-maker for the miracle-workers teachers might yet become." *-From the Foreword by William Ayers*

"A beautifully written quest for meaning through teaching, this narrative imparts a glow and significance to the relation between teachers and learners that can only arise in an awareness of a darkness ordinarily denied. A fine and unusual book, authentic and wise." *-Maxine Greene, Professor of Education (emerita), Teachers College, Columbia University*

"A splendid meditation on education. Feuerverger reminds us of the deepest consulation of the Classroom" *- Richard Rodriguez, author of Hunger of Memory: The Education of Richard Rodriguez*

Transgressions: Cultural Studies and Education volume 5
ISBN 978-90-8790-003-8 (Hardback) ISBN 978-90-8790-000-7 (Paperback)

COUNSELING YOUTH
Foucault, Power and the Ethics of Subjectivity

Tina Besley
University of Illinois at Urbana-Champaign, USA

Using the work of Foucault, this study examines
changing notions of the self and identity and how
psychological and sociological discourses have
conceptualized and constituted adolescence/youth as
the primary client in school counseling. Case studies of
mental hygiene films in the United States and a moral
panic in New Zealand are used to examine how youth
were morally constituted in the postwar period--a time when guidance counseling
emerged in Western countries such as the United States, the United Kingdom,
Australia, Canada, and New Zealand. The author uses Foucault's notion of
governmentality to critically examine how counseling professionalized itself as a
disciplinary body.

This book is targeted at practicing counselors, counseling students and
counselor theoreticians. It will also find audiences with graduate students in youth
studies and those interested in the work and applications of Michel Foucault.

*One of the best things that I can say about this book is that it had a personal
impact. It nudged me into re-thinking various aspects of my work. It is a book that
achieves a rare thing. It talks about counseling young people without getting so
caught up in the detail of practice that it loses sight of the big picture ...I believe
that school counselors who engage with this work will find that their practice is
never quite the same again. They will be invited to think about things they have
previously taken for granted and to listen to young people in new ways.*

John Winslade, Coordinator of Counselor Education, California State University
San Bernardino. Co-Author of Narrative Counseling in Schools: Powerful & Brief.

ISBN 978-90-77874-11-0 (paperback)

Lightning Source UK Ltd.
Milton Keynes UK
173747UK00001BA/18/A